POTTER CRAFT

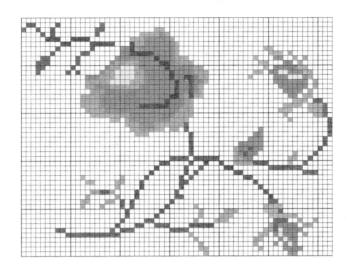

cross-stitch

cross-stitch

techniques • projects • patterns • motifs

Gloria Nicol

Photography by Debbie Patterson

POTTER
CRAFT

New York

Text, design, and layout copyright © 1995 Quadrille Publishing Limited
Project photography copyright © 1995 Debbie Patterson
Detail photography copyright © 1995 Dave King

Published in the United States by Potter Craft,
an imprint of the Crown Publishing Group,
a division of Random House, Inc., New York.
www.crownpublishing.com
www.clarksonpotter.com

POTTER CRAFT and CLARKSON N. POTTER are trademarks and POTTER and colophon are
registered trademarks of Random House, Inc.

Originally published in Great Britain by Quadrille Publishing Limited, London, and in the United
States by Clarkson Potter / Publishers, an imprint of the Crown Publishing Group, a division of
Random House, Inc., New York, in 1995.

Library of Congress Cataloging-in-Publication Data is available.

ISBN–10: 0-307-33964-5
ISBN–13: 978-0-307-33964-5

Printed in China

Cover design by Laura Palese

10 9 8 7 6 5 4 3 2 1

First Potter Craft Edition

contents

Introduction

Cross-stitch must surely be the most versatile of embroidery stitches. This simple stitch can be used entirely alone to make decorative borders, motifs, and panels to embellish plain fabrics. There is something particularly satisfying about working the stitch. The two actions which form each stitch create a perfect and pleasing symmetry, which can be repeated to build up dense shapes and solid blocks of color, or can be applied to form fine curved and twining lines or delicate openwork patterns .

The first crudely worked cross-stitches were used to join animal skins together to provide basic clothing and shelter. From these humble beginnings the stitchers craft developed and over many centuries evolved from a purely practical method of constructing garments to the highly decorative and ornamental process we know today. The perishability of natural fibers has meant that few examples of early stitching have survived but cloth fragments found at archaeological sites in Egypt dating from about AD500 show the use of cross-stitch to decorate the fabric.

Through the ages cross-stitch has become an important part of the folk-art and craft heritage all around the world. Distinctive pattern and colour variations have developed that are particular to specific countries. In China, cross-stitch was almost always worked in dark blue thread on white gauze-like clothing fabric. The European style of embroidery became established during the sixteenth century with brightly dyed threads in red and blue as the predominant colors, often with the addition of brown and black to give outline definition and striking results. Many of these regional variations overlap to create designs that have a universal appeal.

With only one stitch to master and the minimum of materials required, it doesn't take long to become a proficient stitcher. Levels of ability really depend on how much patience the stitcher is blessed with. In essence cross-stitch is not at all complicated, but does require staying power in varying amounts to complete the more densely stitched, elaborate pieces. Over the pages that follow you will find a selection of contemporary and traditional designs that appeal to all different levels of skill and stitching ability.

Beginning cross-stitch

Counted cross-stitch was one of the traditional peasant embroideries of Europe which was successfully used to decorate many different types of articles, from household linens to everyday clothing. Cross-stitches are formed on the right side of the fabric in two parts, a diagonal foundation stitch on the bottom and a diagonal cover stitch on the top; this makes it an easy stitch to learn, as well as to work. Remember to work each cover stitch slanting in the same direction for a smooth and uniform appearance, being careful not to pierce the fabric threads as you stitch. Practice will help you to achieve beautifully formed crosses which can then be worked into the charming designs which you will find in this book.

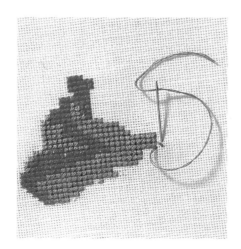

materials

A fine selection of equipment and materials is available for working cross-stitch designs. When choosing a fabric, consider whether the finished product needs to be strong and hardwearing, fine and delicate, plain or patterned. Look for fabrics in your local store and study the new ranges of scissors, needles, and embroidery frames. Take advantage of the wide range of embroidery threads which come in a glorious palette of colors.

Fabrics

Fabrics that make the most suitable background for cross-stitch are of an even weave. On this type of fabric the number of threads running vertically (warp) exactly matches the number of threads running horizontally (weft) and the resulting mesh provides an even grid of regularly spaced holes for the needle to pass through. The number of fabric threads, or "blocks" of threads over a square of 2.5cm (1") is called the "count" of the fabric and is a vital consideration when embarking on any cross-stitch project. The finer the fabric the higher the thread count; the coarser the fabric, the lower the thread count (see Stitches and thread counts, opposite).

A fine fabric with a high thread count will produce smaller stitches and therefore provide the opportunity for more intricate patterning than a coarser weave. A coarser fabric, with a low thread count, will produce larger stitches.

Even-weave linen and cotton produced specifically for counted thread work are the fabrics normally used for cross-stitch. They can be very expensive, however, fabrics for cross-stitch are available in craft and needlework stores, in smaller cut pieces, so look for the size you need, rather than buying full widths of fabric by the yard (meter).

Linen

For centuries, linen, woven with long continuous threads, has been the fabric chosen for making household linens and it is still favored for its strength and hard wearing qualities. Although expensive to buy, it is well worth the investment and when embellished with cross-stitches can produce exquisite results with the enduring quality of an heirloom. It is available in a wide range of thread counts from coarse and heavy to extremely fine.

Cotton

Hardanger is a cotton fabric woven with warp and weft threads that are arranged evenly in pairs. This gives a more accentuated mesh on which to work and the holes are far easier to see.

Aida is similar to hardanger but the warp and weft threads are woven in denser groups, producing an even and accentuated weave that is particularly easy to stitch. Aida is ideal for the beginner.

Checkered fabric has an inherent pattern that makes a regular grid to follow in the same way as the holes on an even-weave fabric and is also a suitable background for working cross-stitch.

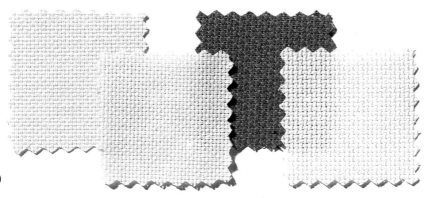

Fabrics with uneven weave

It is possible to work cross-stitch patterns on other fabrics with closer uneven weaves, such as chambray or poplin, by using waste canvas or a piece of even-weave fabric as a guide.

Waste canvas is available in four different thread counts, from 8 to 16, and is worked with a pointed crewel (embroidery) needle. This is an ideal way to add cross-stitch to any fabric. It works best for isolated motifs but it can also be used for borders. It is particularly good for working monograms, which can be placed at an angle to the grain of the fabric (see Using waste canvas on page 17).

Stitches and thread counts

The thread count determines the finished size of the pattern when it is translated from the chart to the fabric; it also dictates the weight and number of strands of thread needed (see Threads, below). For linens and other fabrics with high counts of between 25 and 55 threads per 1" (2.5cm), the cross-stitches are often worked over two or three fabric threads at a time. This means that if the stitches are worked over two threads at a time on a 28 count fabric, a design with 14 stitches per 1" (2.5cm) will result.

Threads For cross-stitch, embroidery threads made from cotton, wool, and silk are most commonly used. Most of the projects in this book are worked using cotton floss, which is available in a vast range of lustrous colors. It is sold in small skeins made up of six fine strands loosely twisted together. Before use, the floss is separated into single strands and re-formed with one or more strands to the thickness required. The floss can be pulled directly from the skein as you work, or it can be cut into lengths and arranged on a piece of cardboard with eyelet holes to hold them neatly in place. Cut maximum lengths of thread between 18" (45cm) and 24" (60cm), as threads that are too long are likely to become tangled. When working with soft embroidery or pearl cotton, use the thread, as it is, straight from the skein.

Number of strands

The fabric thread count dictates the number of strands of floss used (details are given for each project). Use the following guide when designing your own projects.

number of stitches to 1" (2.5cm)	number of strands of cotton floss	size of needle
9	3	24
11	2 or 3	24
14	2	24 or 26
18	1 or 2	26
22	1	26

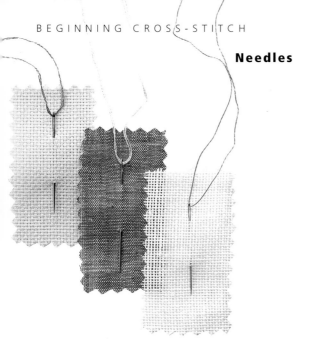

Needles

Blunt-ended tapestry needles are used to make stitches on even-weave fabric, as these push the fabric threads apart without splitting them. The needle should relate to the size of the holes in the fabric mesh – it should slip easily through the fabric without forcing the fabric out of shape, but should be large enough to be held in place by the mesh and not fall through when pushed into the spaces between the threads. The stitch count chart shown on page 11 recommends tapestry needle sizes for a specific number of stitches per 1" (2.5cm).

Counted cross-stitch is always worked with a tapestry needle except when the fabric requires a pointed needle to be used. Crewel (embroidery) needles are needed on waste canvas to pierce the closely woven fabric underneath. They are also used for working woven check or textured fabric, such as the linen huck on pages 86–87. Crewel (embroidery) needles come in sizes numbered from 1 to 10. The following chart shows the right size of needle to use with each different weight of fabric.

fabric	number of strands of cotton floss	crewel (embroidery) needle size
fine lawn	1 or 2	8
medium lawn, sailcloth	3	7
heavier fabric	4 or pearl cotton	6

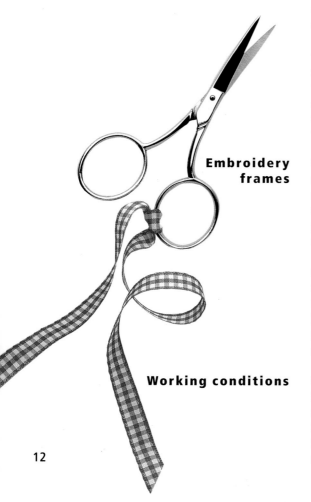

Scissors

A pair of good embroidery scissors is a worthwhile investment and an essential tool for cross-stitch work. They can also be extremely decorative; antique scissors are a highly collectible and coveted tool of the craft.

The scissors should be small and the blades must end in sharp points that can cut the threads close to the fabric, efficiently and cleanly. On the rare occasions when it is necessary to rip out mistakes, these sharp points really come into their own. It is a good idea to tie a piece of colored ribbon to the scissors, so that they are easy to distinguish among colored embroidery threads and to find if they slip from your lap while you are stitching. Keep them especially for the purpose for which they are intended; do *not* be tempted to cut paper with them or the blades will quickly become dull.

Embroidery frames

Unlike needlepoint, where the stitches completely hide the canvas, cross-stitch only covers specific areas and the background fabric is meant to show in some places. This means that the stitches are less likely to distort the fabric, making the use of an embroidery frame unnecessary. Whether you decide to use one or not is therefore a matter of personal preference. With a frame the needle is used at a different angle, so it may be a matter of practicing to find which method suits you best.

Small, round hand frames, used in pairs, can squash and distort those stitches that are pressed between the two wooden hoops. If you like to work with a frame of this type, it is worth completely covering the hoops with fabric binding tape; you will find that this gives the fabric stretched between the frame something more to adhere to and it also allows the hoops to be fastened less tightly. It is wise to remember to remove the frame before putting away the work each time, otherwise the fabric will lose its shape and become difficult to work with later.

Working conditions

Work in daylight whenever possible and in good, soft, artificial light at other times. Daylight simulation light bulbs are inexpensive to buy and are available from art supply stores and good hardware stores. You will find these kinder to the eyes than common household light bulbs and you will notice that colors, particularly threads of similar tones, are easier to distinguish under this light. Attractive workbaskets are widely available to safely store your equipment in when not in use.

working the stitches

Cross-stitch is an easy stitch to work and with only the minimum of practice the basic technique can be mastered quickly. If you are a complete beginner, it is well worth taking some time to learn how to make the stitches correctly and thus form good stitching habits which right from the start, will result in neat, even work. Two simple movements are needed to form each stitch, which soon become second nature, and as stitching becomes quicker and easier it is very encouraging to see beautiful patterns developing on the fabric.

Cross-stitch

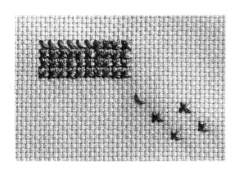

Generally, cross-stitches to form blocks of a single color are worked in rows. A row of half stitches is made in one direction across the fabric and is then completed by crossing back over the stitches in the opposite direction. Most cross-stitch designs can be worked in this way, so areas of pattern are filled in quickly, alternatively, work each single stitch, one at a time. Complex and multicolored designs, requiring isolated stitches in single colors, need to be worked in this way, as do stitches worked over a single fabric thread.

Whether the stitches are worked in rows or singly, the slant of the top stitch should run in the same direction throughout. The only exception to this is when working patterns made up of blocks of quartered motifs, such as the two square pillows on page 26, where each part of the block points toward the center. These can be worked by completing one segment of the motif, then rotating the fabric through a quarter turn to work the next segment, and so on, so that the stitches are formed around the center.

fig 1   fig 2

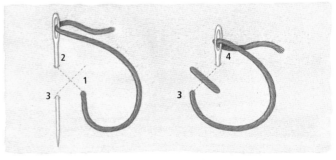

fig 3   fig 4

Working crosses in rows:
1 Work from left to right, laying down half the crosses in a row (fig 1).
2 Work from right to left, inserting the needle at 1 and coming up at 2 (fig 2).

To start a thread
If you are working a block of stitches, hold the end of a short length of thread at the back so that the stitches you are

To finish off a thread
At the end of a color block, or when the thread is getting too short, pull it through to the back and run the needle under a few stitches of the same color to hold it firmly in place. Then clip the thread end close to the fabric to keep the back neat.

Working crosses singly:
1 Bring the needle up at 1, insert at 2, and come up at 3, under 2 (fig 3).
2 Bring the needle up at 1 and insert at 4 to cover the foundation stitch (fig 4).

making will catch it. When working only a few stitches in one color, catch the thread underneath a few stitches of another color on the back.

When blocks stitched in the same color are only a short distance apart, strand the thread behind other stitches across the back of the work for continuous stitching. When using finely woven fabrics dark threads can show through on the front, so keep these "bridging" threads short.

The reverse side

Great emphasis is often placed on the neatness of the back of the embroidery and there are certainly aesthetic advantages in this, especially when it may sometimes be visible, such as on a towel border or along a sheet border. In these cases the back of the work should be made up of small straight stitches arranged in neat parallel lines. The back of the stitches on pillows and samplers is not so crucial, as they will be hidden from view. Do not sacrifice enthusiasm and spontaneity by worrying about such refinements, but again, a little time spent developing a good, even technique is likely to pay off by producing neat stitches on both sides – as a general rule, the condition of the back of the work is a reflection of the quality of the front.

Ripping stitches

If you make a mistake, only rip out the stitches if you really have to: when hidden within a patterned panel or densely worked area, a block of stitches sloping in the wrong direction may not be noticeable to anyone but you. If stitches must be taken out, take care that the fabric threads are not pulled out of line and the holes in the mesh do not become enlarged. Use pointed scissors to cut the thread frequently, so that the strands pulled out are kept short and are therefore easy to remove.

Backstitch

Backstitch can be used to outline a pattern and to add definition to a design, as well as in its own right. This versatile stitch can be worked in all directions to make horizontal and vertical lines as well as diagonals. It helps to break up areas of stitching that might otherwise look too dense and can be used without becoming overpowering. Antique cross-stitch sampler designs, often have letters of the alphabet outlined in backstitch.

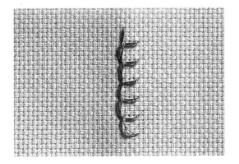

Working the stitch
Using one strand of floss, bring the needle and thread from the back up through the fabric in the first hole. Push the needle back down into the fabric two threads along, at the same time pointing it forward so that it pushes up through the fabric two threads or more in front of the new stitch. Take a small stitch backward into the last stitch worked, over as many threads as required, these will generally match the depth of the cross-stitches.

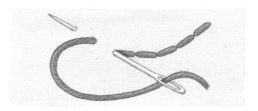

Blanket stitch

Using blanket stitch to finish off a hem is a simple way to add an extra decorative touch to your needlework. As well as edging blankets, such as the crib blanket on page 36, the stitch can be used in contrasting or complementary colors to embellish the borders of pillowcases (page 34) and tablecloth hems (pages 40 and 44).

Working from left to right, keep the stitches the same depth throughout to make a straight and even border.

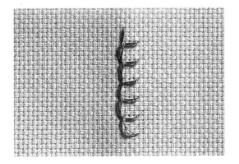

Working the stitch
1 Join the thread to the outside edge and bring the needle over and down into the fabric above this point and slightly to the right of it.
2 Point the needle down the back of the fabric toward the edge and pull it evenly through the loop made by the thread. Repeat, keeping the stitches evenly spaced as you work.

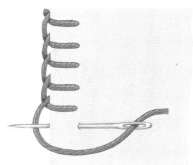

starting

A little time and thought spent in preparation before starting will save you trouble later. Keep the work crease free and clean and always be generous when cutting out, allowing extra fabric all the way around because a larger piece will be easier to work with. Carefully center the motif or position the border to ensure a successful finish to your work.

Preparation

Inspect the fabric to be used and iron out any creases before beginning to sew. Avoid fabric that has been folded for some time, as the outside edges of long-standing creases often become stained. If the fabric is soiled, cut it to size avoiding the marks or, if this is impossible, wash it before you begin.

Try to keep the fabric clean while you work – it will save a lot of trouble later on. Wash your hands frequently as you stitch so that the natural oils in your skin do not soil the work, and store it in a workbasket between stitching sessions to help to keep it looking fresh. The fabric will inevitably become crumpled, but can quickly be restored to its original condition by ironing when stitching is complete.

Cutting out

Always cut a piece of fabric larger than is needed for the finished piece; it can be cut down to the correct size when the work is finished. With even-weave fabrics the piece can be cut lengthwise or widthwise without any appreciable difference in quality, so use whichever way will be most economical. If the project is likely to take some time to complete, it is worth turning under or zigzag stitching the raw edges on a sewing machine to prevent them from unraveling. In every project in the book extra fabric has been allowed for trimming to size later.

Positioning the design

The pattern stitches will be applied by working from the middle of the fabric out toward the edges and the design therefore needs to be placed centrally. In order to do this, you will need to mark the center of the fabric with lines of basting stitches.

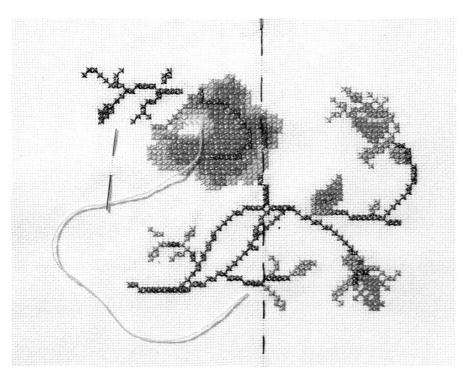

1 Start by folding the piece of fabric in half lengthwise and mark the line made by the fold with a pin. Work a row of basting stitches along the fold line, following the grain of the fabric made by a warp thread.

2 Next, fold the fabric in half widthwise and in the same way as in step 1, mark along the resulting fold with basting stitches. This time you will be following the line of the weft thread.

Occasionally, it will be necessary to plot a border pattern running around the edges of the design, before you position the central motif or pattern.

If it is necessary to count fabric threads over a large area, you will find it helpful to place pins at 10-stitch intervals. You will be surprised how much quicker and easier it is for you to keep count in this way. If you use this method, take care that the weave of the threads does not become distorted by the pins.

Working the design

The central point and guide lines are now clearly visible for you to begin working the design, following the chart that you have chosen.

Where a motif appears in isolation, it may be easier to mark its position using basting thread or, a special marking pen, sold for embroidery purposes, which will lightly mark the fabric but disappears in the first wash.

Following a chart

It is important to understand that each square on a chart represents one cross-stitch on the fabric. No matter how many fabric threads a cross-stitch is worked over, it is always represented by only one square on the chart. The color of each square corresponds to a color given in the color key beside each chart, with shade numbers to indicate the exact colors to use in each case. The thread colors listed for each project are given in two widely available brands, Anchor and DMC.

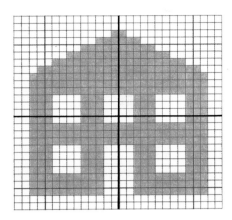

Using waste canvas

1 Cut a piece of waste canvas 2"–3" (5-7cm) bigger all around than the design you wish to stitch.

2 Place the canvas on your fabric where the design is required. Follow the grain of the fabric unless stated otherwise. To prevent the canvas slipping as well as to mark the central threads for placement of the design, baste it securely in place, with lines of stitching making a cross at the center as well as around the edges of the canvas. For larger designs, extra lines of basting may be necessary to secure the canvas in place.

3 Beginning at the center in the usual way, work the design by stitching into the holes of the canvas and through the fabric beneath, taking care that the needle goes cleanly into the holes and does not pierce the threads of the canvas (pierced threads can be difficult to remove later). Use the number of strands of floss to cor-

respond to the appropriate thread count as normal.

4 When the stitching is complete, remove all the basting threads and trim the waste canvas to within 1" (2.5cm) of the stitched area on all sides. Dampen the waste fabric threads until they become limp and then pull them out of the canvas, thread by thread. You may need to use tweezers to do this. Be sure to draw them out close to the fabric and only in the direction in which the canvas threads lie. To remove long threads of waste canvas when working larger designs, it may be helpful to cut the waste canvas threads between areas of stitching.

Even-weave fabric can be used in the same way as waste canvas and does not require dampening before removing the threads. Take particular care that the threads are not pierced by the needle when stitching if using even-weave fabric as your guide.

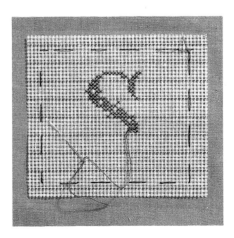

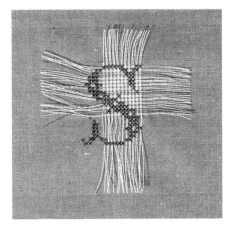

finishing off

When a completed piece has been carefully and painstakingly worked, it is well worth taking the time to make the finishing touches extra special to show off your talent to best advantage. Adding drawn thread work hems to tablecloths and bed linen gives them a distinctive quality with a traditional character. Mitered corners give an elegant, smooth finish to the right side of the work and have the advantage of looking so much more professional than hems that are simply turned under.

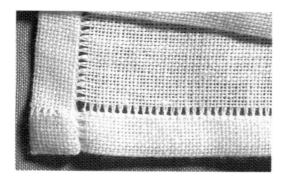

Drawn thread work hem

1 Work out the position of the hem edge and hem line and mark with pins.
2 Pull two of the threads out of the fabric following the hem line, to leave an open band of adjacent threads.
3 Turn up the hem to meet the edge of the drawn threads. Next, pin and baste in place (fig 1).

4 Using a length of sewing thread and a sharp needle, and with the wrong side of the work facing you, bring the needle up through the threads and work the stitches in sequence, catching the hem in place (fig 2). Continue in this way, at the same time pulling the threads of the open band together so as to create a regular and decorative hem.

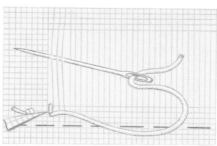

fig 1

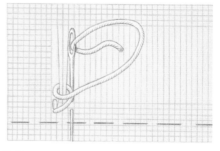

fig 2

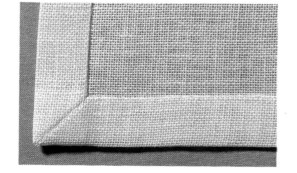

Mitering a corner

1 Along each raw edge, turn under a hem of an equal depth of fabric and press to mark the folds (fig 3).
2 Turn under a slightly larger hem to conceal any raw edges completely and press again in the same way.
3 Pin, then baste the hem in place to within 4" (10cm) of each corner.
4 Unfold the hem at each corner, revealing the pressed fold lines. Turn under the

corner of the fabric to make a right-angled triangle, with the inside corner point exactly touching the center of the slope of the triangle (fig 4). Press, unfold, and trim close to the diagonal fold.
5 Turn this diagonal fold back into the fabric, then fold the hems back in position to make a flat, mitered corner with sloping edges that meet diagonally along the corner (fig 5). Baste and slipstitch all along the hem edge.

fig 3

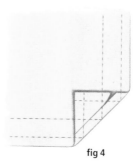

fig 4

fig 5

Caring for your work

When the stitching is completed, hopefully the finished piece will be clean, in which case it will simply need a quick pressing with an iron to revitalize it. When a piece has taken a long time to work, however, it may need to be washed and pressed before it is used or framed.

In the past it was generally recommended that luke warm water and mild detergent without bleach be used, and that the fabric be washed gently without rubbing, rinsed well, and dried flat on a towel. Nowadays, the main manufacturers of embroidery threads tend to advise rather more robust treatment, as the threads are dyed to be colorfast and they launder best in a washing machine with as high a temperature as the fabric will stand, up to 200°F. This certainly has advantages for everyday household linens, which will require many washes throughout their life.

When ironing cross-stitch, the iron should never be applied to the right side of the work as this will flatten and spoil the stitches. Instead, place several layers of towels on the ironing board, lay the cross-stitched piece face down on them, and cover with another piece of fabric. Use the iron at the linen setting and press the work while it is just damp. This way, the stitches will retain their slightly embossed look.

Keep the finished piece out of direct sunlight whenever possible to help prevent the threads losing their vibrancy.

Aging the fabric

Antique linens have a character that is impossible to copy authentically but can be recreated, giving new household items an heirloom quality. Old samplers that have faded and mellowed with time have a particular charm that can be mimicked by matching the subtle colorings of the worn threads and fabrics, while tea is used to "age" new linen.

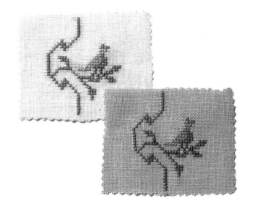

1 Choose ivory and natural linen and cotton fabrics to achieve the best results.
2 Wash the fabric to remove any dressing that might have been applied to its surface during manufacture.
3 Make a pot of tea and leave it to brew in the usual way.
4 When the tea is cold, strain the liquid into a bowl and insert the linen. Soak for about 10 minutes, stirring occasionally.
5 Allow the fabric to drip dry naturally and iron out any creases before you begin to stitch.

Finished samplers can be treated in the same way to take any harshness away from the colors of threads and background fabric, but you will require a strong nerve when the stitched piece has taken a long time to work. Experiment first with a spare piece of background fabric worked with a few stitches.

Tea-dip aging is only really suitable for decorative pieces that will not require washing. Make sure that all threads used are colorfast before attempting to use this technique!

Stretching and framing samplers and pictures

Before the finished work is framed it needs to be stretched over a piece of cardboard to hold it flat and taut. A professional framer will be able to do this for you, but it is quite easy to do it yourself and will be considerably cheaper.

You will need a piece of acid-free cardboard over which to stretch the work. This should be the same size as the design, plus an allowance for a narrow plain border all around the design for the frame rebate.

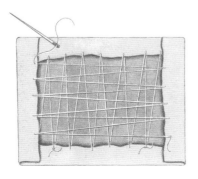

1 Iron the work on the wrong side, as described in caring for your work.
2 The backing card needs to be the same size as the glass.
3 Cut the card and place to the wrong side of the sampler.

4 Fold the fabric over the cardboard so that the embroidered area is centered.
5 Lace the back together with strong thread to hold it firmly in place.
6 Sew the long sides first, checking the final position, then work the short sides.

In the bedroom

Hand-stitched bed linen is always a delight, both to see, and to use. Among this collection of beautiful bed linen, you will find a wide selection of attractive designs to suit a variety of tastes. The simple crib blanket with nursery motifs, to make for a special baby, is an ideal choice for the novice as it is worked freehand in a slightly thicker thread.

The experienced embroiderer might appreciate something more elaborate to stitch, and the beautiful sheet border will offer this opportunity. An intricate floral pattern, worked in a wide color range, makes this a delicate addition to any bedroom. Alternatively, a simple motif combined with a monogrammed initial, adds special style to the Oxford pillowcases.

sheet border

A verdant border of cottage-garden roses makes a splendid edging for a sheet border. Such dense stitching requires patience and experience, but the result is well worth the effort – transforming an everyday item into an heirloom. The border is designed to drape across the top of the bed and is not attached to the sheet, so it will require less washing than the rest of the bed linen and this will help to keep the embroidery in good condition. A heavy lace crocheted edging balances well with the strength and vibrancy of the floral design. You may even be lucky and find antique lace that is in good enough condition to use. The sheet border is stitched from the center outward, so it can be made to fit any size of bed.

About the border

Approximate finished size: 78" x 41" (198 x 104cm), excluding lace edging
Size of one motif: 13½" x 7¼" (34 x 18.5cm)
Number of stitches per 1" (2.5cm): 14
Work stitches over two threads at a time when using fabric with double the thread count

You will need

2½yd (2.2m) white linen, 55"(140cm) wide, 28 threads per 1" (2.5cm)
2yd (2m) lace edging
Tapestry needle size 24 or 26
Cotton embroidery floss in the colors specified on page 24 or 25.
Use two strands of floss throughout.

To work the design

1 Mark the position for the placement of the center motif by folding the fabric in half widthwise. Make a row of basting stitches along the fold to mark the center, following the line of the warp threads.
2 Measure 7" (18cm) in from the edge of the fabric and make a short row of basting stitches, following the line of the weft threads, to intersect the center fold line. This line marks the position of the bottom of the sheet border. Count 102 threads and make another row of basting stitches, following the weft threads; this new line marks the top edge of the border.
3 Matching the center line marked on the chart to the line of basting along the center of the fabric, work the first motif.
4 Working outward from the center, continue to stitch the rest of the border design until five motifs have been completed (two either side of the center one). If you have altered the size of the border you will also need to adjust the number of motifs worked.
5 Work another half motif at either end of the border.

To finish

1 Trim the fabric to size. First, measure 5" (12.5cm) down from the bottom of the border, mark with pins, and cut the fabric straight following the line of the weft threads. Next, measure 31¼" (75cm) up from the top of the border, mark with pins, and cut the fabric, following the line of the weft threads. For the side edges, measure 40" (101cm) both ways from the center fold line, mark with pins and cut the fabric straight, along the line of the warp threads.
2 Press under ⅜" (1cm) to the wrong side along the bottom edge, then turn under a 1" (2.5cm) hem. Stitch in position either by hand or by machine. If you wish, you can work a decorative drawn thread work hem, following the technique shown on page 18. This will give a more elegant finish to the border.
3 Turn under ⅜" (1cm) turnings, followed by ⅜" (1cm) hems, along the other three sides of the border. Stitch in place, mitering the corners if required (see page 18).
4 Pin the lace along the edge of the lower hem, baste, and slipstitch it neatly in place to complete the sheet border.
5 Carefully press the border on the wrong side to complete.

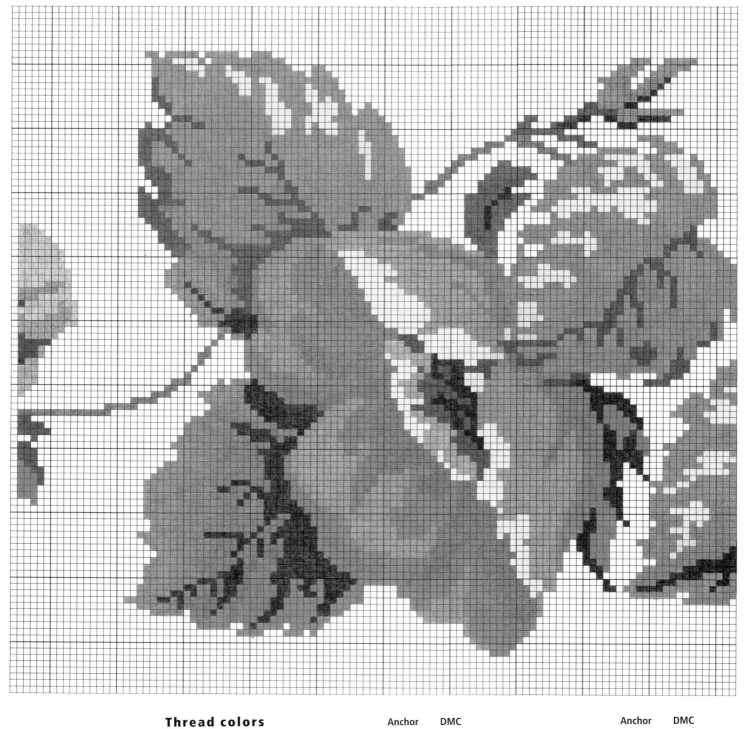

Thread colors

		Anchor	DMC			Anchor	DMC
☐	cream	366	739	▨	red	46	666
☐	yellow	301	745	▨	rose	75	962
▨	peach	9	352	▨	magenta	89	917
▨	rust	1049	3826	▨	pale lilac	108	210

		Anchor	DMC			Anchor	DMC			Anchor	DMC
	lilac	109	209		blue	187	3814		brown	358	801
	purple	98	553		pale green	244	987		black	403	310
	dark purple	101	550		leaf green	188	943				
	pale blue	186	993		bottle green	683	890				

square bed pillows

Big and luxurious bed pillows make a decorative feature in a room, as well as providing a comfortable back rest for reading or breakfasting in bed. The cross-stitch designs for both these pillows are made up of square motifs, worked in sequence to build up dense areas of colorful pattern onto the antique linen background. This type of patterning offers plenty of scope for variation and adaptation; you can arrange the same motifs in many different ways: they could be worked in rows around the pillow, to make deeper borders, or alternated, to create a checkerboard effect. For a classic finishing touch, the pillows are fastened at the back, with pearl buttons.

About the pillows

Star pillow (pages 28-29)
Approximate size: 28" (71cm) square
Number of stitches per 1" (2.5cm): 11
Flower pillow (pages 30–31)
Approximate size: 24½" (62cm) square
Number of stitches per 1" (2.5cm): 18
Work stitches over two threads at a time when using fabric with double the thread count.

Star pillow

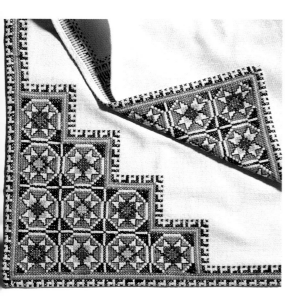

You will need

1¾yd (1.7m) antique white hardanger,
55" (140cm) wide, 22 threads per
1" (2.5cm)
6 pearl buttons, ¾" (2cm) in diameter
Pillow form 21", (71cm) square approx
Tapestry needle size 24 or 26
Cotton embroidery floss in the colors
specified below
Use two strands of floss throughout

To work the design

1 For the pillow front, cut a piece of fabric 33" (87cm) square. Position the central diamond pattern by folding the fabric in half, lengthwise then widthwise. Mark the folds with rows of basting stitches that cross at the center point. Follow the line of the fabric threads.

2 Matching the center point marked on the chart to the center point marked on the fabric, work the diamond arrangement of star motifs as placed, following the color chart until it is complete. Where indicated on the chart, work outline stitches in backstitch (see page15) around the motifs.

3 Leaving a band of plain fabric, 3½" (8cm) wide all around, begin at one corner and work the narrow border pattern, followed by the corner blocks of star motifs as shown on the chart.

4 Trim the pillow front to size, leaving a seam allowance of ⅝" (1.5cm) on each side. The pillow front should now measure 29¼" (74cm) square.

To finish

1 For the pillow back, cut two rectangles of fabric: a small one measuring 29¼" x 10¼" (74 x 26cm) and a large one measuring 29¼" x 26" (74 x 65.5cm).

2 Stitch together the pillow following the instructions on page 30.

Thread colors

		Anchor	DMC
	pink	76	961
	yellow	289	307
	green	257	905
	blue	164	824
	black	403	310

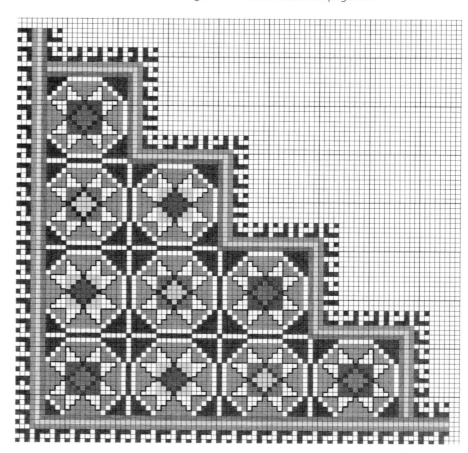

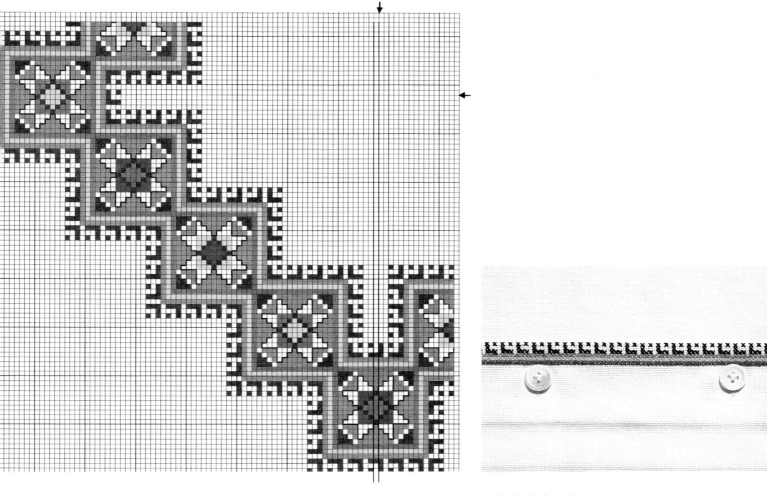

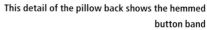

This detail of the pillow back shows the hemmed button band

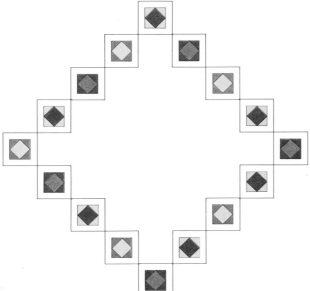

Flower pillow

You will need

1¾yd (1.5m) antique white Edinburg linen, 55" (140cm) wide, 36 threads per 1" (2.5cm)

6 pearl buttons, ¾" (2cm) diameter

Pillow form, 24½" (62cm) square approx

Tapestry needle size 24 or 26

Cotton embroidery floss in the colors specified on page 32

Use two strands of floss throughout

To work the design

1 Cut a piece of fabric 29½" (78cm) square for the pillow front. Mark the center of each side by folding the fabric, and then work a line of basting stitches, approximately 8" (20cm) long, at right angles to the edges of the fabric.

2 Leaving a 4" (9cm) edge of fabric all the way around the outside, begin at one corner and, working outward, stitch the narrow border pattern. Work first in one direction to the center of one side, then in the other direction to the center of the other side, following the line of the fabric threads. Work from the other three corners in the same way until the border is completed all around the pillow. The bud

patterns slant diagonally in toward the center. Make any adjustments necessary where the borders meet. Work outline stitches in backstitch (see page15) on motifs as indicated on the chart.

3 Next, work the corner motifs within the border, following the chart.

4 Work the arrangement of three motifs, placing them centrally along each side of the pillow.

5 Trim the front to size, leaving a ⅜" (1cm) band of unstitched fabric all around the embroidered border, plus a seam allowance of ⅝" (1.5cm) on all sides. The pillow front should now measure 25¾" (65cm) square.

To finish

1 For the pillow back, cut a rectangle of fabric 25¾" x 10¾" (65 x 26cm) and another one 25¾" x 22½" (65 x 56.5cm)

2 Stitch together the pillow following the instructions below.

3 Decorate the edge of the pillow with closely worked rows of blanket stitch (see page 15) or work a narrow border of crochet if preferred.

To stitch together the finished pillows

Stitch the pillows after the designs have been worked on to the fronts. Both pillows are stitched in the same way.

1 Prepare the pieces for the back of the pillow. Taking the smaller rectangle, make a hem along one long side, turning under of ⅝" (1.5cm), then 2" (5cm). Baste in position, press, then stitch by hand or machine.

2 Cut and stitch six buttonholes along this hem. Start by marking the holes at each end, 3" (8cm) in from the side, then space the remaining four evenly between them. Work the buttonholes by hand or alternatively using a sewing machine. Make sure that they are big enough to fit the buttons.

3 Hem along one long edge of the large

rectangle for the back, turning under ⅜" (1cm), then ¾" (2cm). Baste in position, press and then stitch together by hand or machine.

4 With right sides together, place the small rectangle on the pillow front, matching raw edges along three sides, and pin in place. Position the larger rectangle on the pillow front in the same way, matching raw edges and ensuring that the hemmed edge overlaps that of the small rectangle. Pin and baste.

5 Stitch around the seams, within the seam allowance and following the grain of the fabric, trim the corners, and turn right side out. Press the edges carefully, taking care not to squash the embroidery.

6 Sew on the buttons to complete.

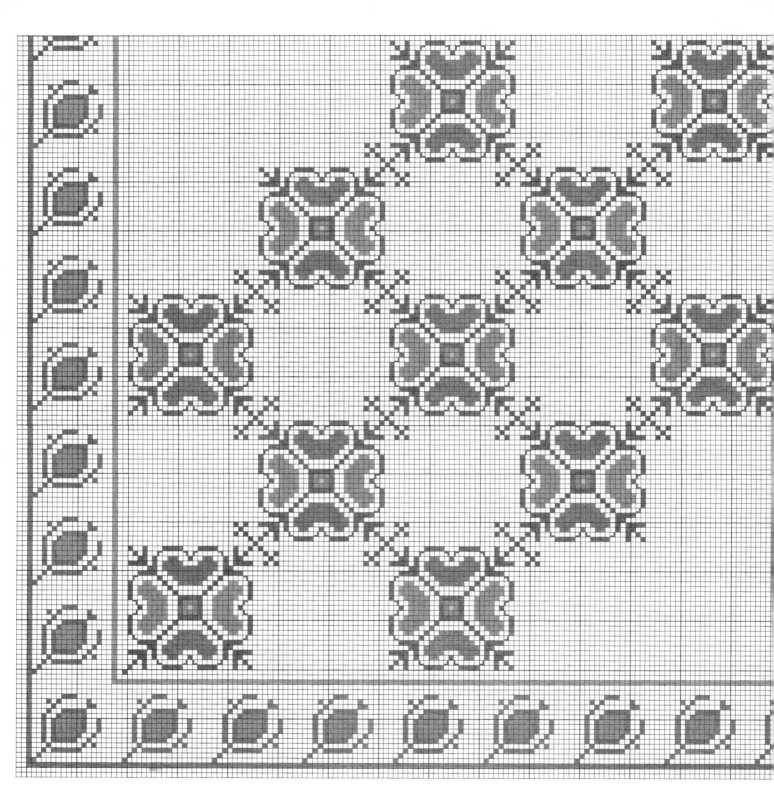

Thread colors

		Anchor	DMC			Anchor	DMC
	pink	42	309		green	244	987
	yellow	313	977		blue	164	824

	Anchor	DMC
brown	905	3781

monogrammed pillowcases

Traditional embroidered monograms add a distinctive flourish to household linens. Worked on waste canvas, they can be used to decorate existing bed linen or attached to cotton or linen fabric after the embroidery is completed; as they require only a small amount of stitching, they are an ideal project for the novice stitcher. Oxford pillowcases like these have a classic style, providing a perfect foil for monograms, and they are surprisingly easy to make. Draw your own monogram following the charted alphabets on pages 98–101; use graph tracing paper to position intertwined letters with elegant sweeping curves linking them together. Alternatively, why not work an alphabet together with a motif such as crowns or keys as shown in the charts on page 105, to give your linen regal appeal.

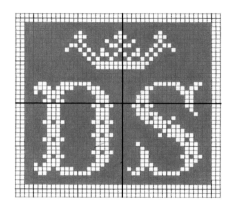

Thread color

	Anchor	DMC
cream	926	822

About the pillowcases

Approximate finished size: 36" x 26" (91cm x 66cm), including 3¼" (8cm) border
Number of stitches per 1" (2.5cm): 10

You will need

For one pillowcase
1¼yd (2.1m) cotton chambray, 44" (112cm) wide
Waste canvas, 10 threads per 1" (2.5cm)
Crewel (embroidery) needle size 7
Cotton embroidery floss in the color specified below
Use three strands of thread throughout

To prepare the fabric and work the design

1 For the front, cut a piece of chambray 37" x 27" (94 x 69cm), following the grain of the fabric. Baste the stitching line for the inside border edge, 3⅝" (9.5cm) from the edges of the fabric and parallel to all four sides of the rectangle. For the back, cut two pieces of fabric: the main piece 33" x 27" (84.5 x 69cm) and the flap 15½" x 27" (35.5 x 69cm).

2 Draw your monogram on graph paper, following the charted alphabets on pages 98–101, and mark the center point by drawing two intersecting lines. Cut a piece of waste canvas, following the threads; make it 2½" (5cm) bigger than the monogram on every side and mark the horizontal and vertical center threads lightly with a pencil.

3 For a centrally placed monogram, mark the center point on the pillowcase front with two lines of intersecting basting stitches (see page 16) or place the monogram elsewhere on the pillowcase,

such as a corner, marking the position with basting stitches running straight or diagonally, as required, to correspond to the horizontal and vertical intersecting lines marked on the chart.

4 Baste the waste canvas in place, matching the pencil lines to the basting stitches on the fabric. Work the monogram from the chart, plotting the letters from the center outward.

5 When stitching is complete, remove the waste canvas threads carefully (see page 17). Press the work lightly.

To finish

1 Turn under ¾" (2cm) to the wrong side, then make a 1½" (3cm) hem along one short edge of the main back piece. Baste and press, then stitch in place. In the same way, make a hem along one long edge on the flap piece, turning under of ⅜" (1cm) to the wrong side then ¾" (2cm).

2 With right sides together, place the back flap on the pillowcase front, matching raw edges along three of the sides. Place the main back piece on the pillowcase front in the same way as before, so that the hemmed edge of the pillowcase overlaps the hemmed edge of the flap, being sure to match raw edges. Pin and baste all around.

3 Stitch around the pillowcase, taking a ⅝" (1.5cm) seam allowance. Trim the corners and turn right side out, then baste close to the outside edge and press. Mark and machine stitch a line 3" (8cm) from all edges to make the border.

4 Remove all basting stitches and carefully press on the wrong side.

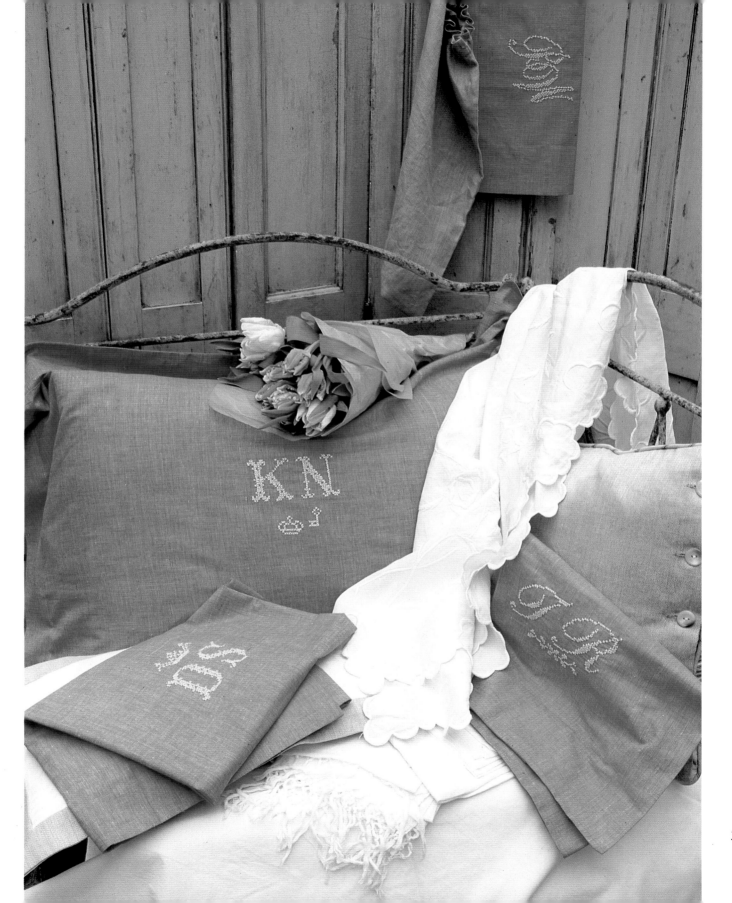

crib blanket

An embroidered blanket, decorated with simple motifs, makes a charming crib cover. Old blankets can be cut to size and bound with blanket stitches in a colored thread, giving them a new lease of life; brand-new blankets work just as well. Choose a classic color and make sure the wool is soft. A simple grid, made from lines worked in freehand cross-stitches, divides the blanket into squares, into which the motifs are placed. Work as few or as many motifs as you like, to make the project simple or more ambitious. Use the number and alphabet motifs shown on pages 98–101, to cover a bigger blanket for a child's bed.

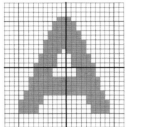

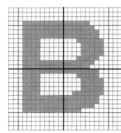

Thread colors

		Anchor	DMC
	coral	10	2356
	blue	168	2826
	dark blue	161	2797
	pink	24	2818
	yellow	293	2743
	lime	0278	2218
	pale green	185	2599
	tan	362	2158
	beige	392	2642

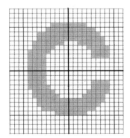

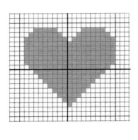

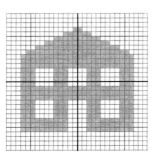

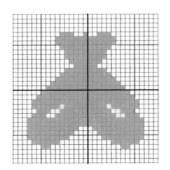

About the blanket

Approximate finished size: 30" x 43"
  (76 x109cm)
Number of stitches per 1" (2.5cm): 8.5

You will need

32" x 45" (0.8m x 113cm) blanket fabric
Waste canvas, 8.5 threads per 1" (2.5cm)
Tapestry needle size 20 or 22
Soft embroidery floss in the colors
  specified left
Use one strand of thread throughout

To prepare the blanket

1 Along each edge of the blanket, make hems by rolling up ³⁄₈" (1cm) of fabric, twice. Baste in place. Using soft embroidery cotton, which has a matt finish and is available in a large range of colors, work blanket stitch (see page 15) all around the blanket edges. Make each stitch large enough to cover the depth of the hem and hold it in place.

2 Divide the width of the blanket into five equal parts and, placing pins at regular intervals, mark four lines down the length of it. Baste beside the pins to mark the lines, then remove the pins. Work even lines of cross stitches over the basted lines, then remove the basting.

3 Divide the length of the blanket into seven equal parts and use pins to mark six lines. Baste, then work cross stitch as in step 2, to form a grid of squares over the whole blanket. Remove the basting.

To work the motifs

Following the charts, work the motifs centrally within the squares (see pictures). Proceed as follows:

1 Cut the waste canvas into 4½" (11cm) squares. Following the line of the threads, lightly mark the central lines with a pencil in both directions.

2 Mark the center of the square to be worked with two lines of basting stitches. Place a piece of waste canvas on the square, matching the center markings, and baste in place. Choose a motif, and plotting it from the center outward work it over the canvas, following the chart.

3 When all the motifs have been worked, remove the waste canvas carefully (see page 17), leaving the embroidered shapes in the squares.

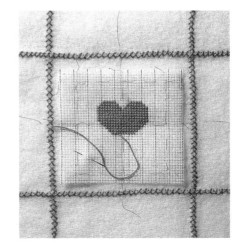

For the table

The selection of designs in this chapter offers something to suit all tastes. Beautifully embroidered table linens set the style and are always a useful item to make. Choose classic rose motifs evoking a summer's day, or alternatively, a blue and white traditional cross-stitch design, reminiscent of Dutch tile work. For lunch al fresco or cozy supper parties, the gingham table mats are a perfect choice. They are decorated with snowflake medallions, which are worked in groups of crosses forming colorful patterns over the gingham squares; a selection of alternative medallion motifs is shown enabling you to work a different one on every mat if you wish. Add the finishing touch to any well-dressed table with these original numbered napkin rings, which will appeal to those who enjoy rather quicker results.

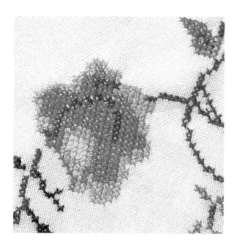

rose tablecloth

Rose flowers and buds are classic motifs, instantly conjuring up the delights of summer gardens and luxuriant arbors, clad with fragrant blooms. When decorated with rose patterns in cross-stitch, table linens will impart a cottage-like atmosphere to your home. They also make the perfect setting for pretty floral china, both for afternoon tea and informal dining. The cloth described here can be adapted to fit any size of table by simply adding more motifs around the edges to suit your own requirements. You will find that the motifs which decorate the border are easy to work. It is worth hemming the tablecloth before you start to work the cross-stitch, as the hemmed edges will stop the fabric from unraveling while stitching is in progress. If looked after well, a fine tablecloth such as this is destined to become a family heirloom.

About the tablecloth

Approximate finished size: 55" (140cm) square

Number of stitches per 1" (2.5cm): 11

Work stitches over two threads at a time when using fabric with double the thread count

You will need

1¾yd (1.5m) even-weave linen, 59" (150cm) wide, 22 threads per 1 (2.5cm)

Tapestry needle size 24 or 26

Cotton embroidery floss in the colors specified on page 42

Use two strands of thread throughout

To prepare the fabric

1 Cut the fabric to 57" (145cm) square. Make a hem all around by turning under ⅜" (1cm) then ⅝" (1.5cm). Miter each corner (see page 18). Pin and baste the hem in position.

2 Secure the hem with slipstitch, then remove the basting.

3 With right sides facing, work cross-stitches all around the edge of the cloth so that, at the back, the cross-stitches catch the top edge of the hem.

To work the design

1 Measure 5" (13cm) in from the edges of the tablecloth, making a square. Mark with pins, then work lines of basting. This defines the outer edge of the border.

2 Fold the square in half and, using the fold lines, mark the center points on two of the sides with a few basting stitches.

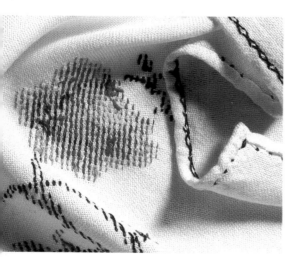

Unfold and repeat for the other sides. Matching the edge line on the chart to the basted border line, work a flower and bud motif on the marked center of each side of the border square.

3 Work a flower and bud motif at each corner, inside the border lines. Position the motif as on the chart, matching the edge and corner lines to the basted lines on the tablecloth.

4 Halve the space between the motifs and mark with basting stitches. Work a long border motif between each flower and bud, matching the edge and central lines on the chart to the basted lines and center markings. Remove basting.

41

5 Fold the tablecloth into quarters to find the center point, and mark it with a pin. Measure 10½" (26cm) out from the center point, along each fold, and again mark with pins. Using the pin markers as a guide, work straight lines of basting stitches to make a 21" (52cm) square in the center of the tablecloth. Leave the pins in place for now.

6 Work a flower and bud motif at each corner of this smaller square, placing them so as to match the edge and corner lines on the chart to the basted lines. Work a short border motif between the flower and bud motifs, matching the edge line to the basted line, and the center line to the pin markers. Remove the pins and basting stitches.

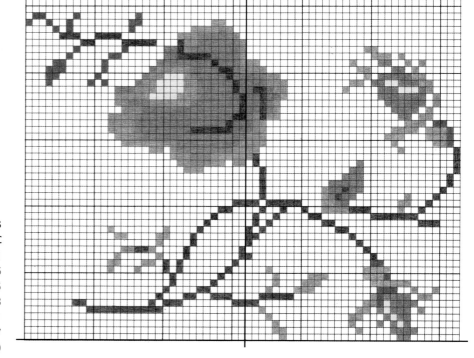

Thread colors

		Anchor	DMC
	red	9046	321
	pink	54	956
	yellow	288	445
	brown	381	938
	dark green	212	561
	bright green	255	907
	royal	134	820

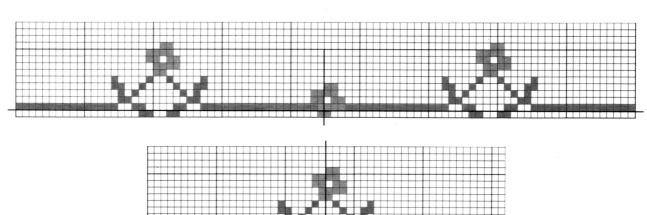

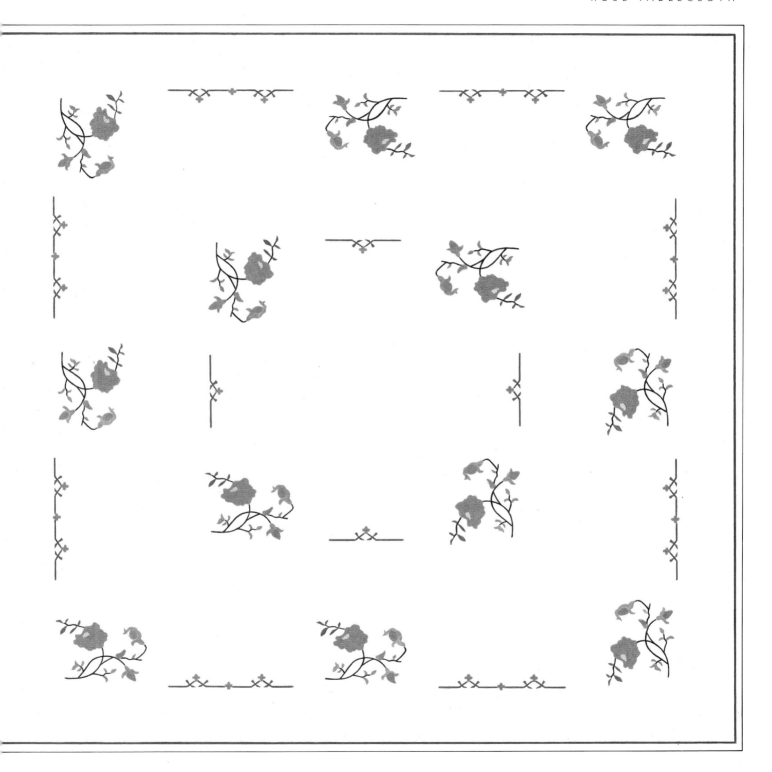

blue and white tablecloth

Blue and white brings a freshness to traditional cross-stitch designs and is an ideal color combination for table linens. Patterns made up of square motifs are versatile and relatively easy to work. Here, an antique cloth has two alternating motifs – a flower and a geometric square – filling each corner. The center panel is decorated with a delicate, open grid.

The original piece was worked with great skill by an experienced stitcher using fine woolen crêpe fabric. For the less experienced, a fine linen, on which the threads are easy to count, is recommended, making the overall effect easier to achieve. Alternatively, the design can be simplified by working on a fabric with a lower thread count, resulting in larger blocks of pattern which will fill the tablecloth much more quickly.

About the tablecloth

Approximate finished size: 39" x 42½" (99 x 108cm)

Number of stitches per 1" (2.5cm): 16

Work stitches over two threads at a time when using fabric with double the thread count

You will need

1½yd (1.2m) even-weave linen, 55" (140 cm) wide, 32 threads per 1" (2.5cm)

Tapestry needle size 24

Cotton embroidery floss in the colors specified on pages 46–47

Use two strands of floss throughout

To work the design

1 Starting from one corner of the fabric, measure 8" (20cm) in from the long edge and 6" (15cm) in from the short edge; mark the fabric with a pin, setting the first corner point. Make lines of basting stitches from this point, following the grain of the fabric, thus marking the outer edges for the positioning of the blocks of motifs along two sides of the tablecloth – one short, one long.

2 Beginning in the corner marked out by basting stitches and starting with a square motif, stitch 27 alternating flower and square motifs in a row, inside the line of basting, along the longer side (see charts). Stitch the flowers facing in toward the center of the tablecloth.

3 Starting from the square motif in the corner, work 11 alternating flower and square motifs in a row, inside the line of basting, along the shorter edge (see charts). Leave a gap of six threads then, beginning with a flower motif, work 12

more motifs, to take you to the next corner point.

4 To complete the border, work rows of motifs on the other two sides of the rectangle to match the two sides already stitched. Fill in the corners with diagonal rows of alternating motifs. Fewer rows of motifs can be worked if required.

5 Fold the tablecloth into quarters, matching the edges of the rectangle made up of square motifs, and use a pin to mark the center point within the patterned area. Work a square motif at the center of the cloth. Following the chart (see pages 46–47), plot out the flower and leaf border design so that it forms a grid around the centrally placed motif. Work a square motif in the middle of the eight other spaces made by the grid.

6 Starting from the corner, work toward the middle, stitching the outer border pattern around the cloth. Where the stitching meets along the sides, make any adjustments necessary to fit the pattern.

To finish

1 Measure 1¼" (3.5cm) from the outside edges of the border on all sides and cut the fabric, following the grain.

2 Turn under hems of ¼" (5mm) followed by ⅜" (1cm), along the long sides of the tablecloth, baste and press. Make drawn thread work hems (see page 18) along both sides.

3 In the same way, turn under hems along the short sides of the tablecloth and make drawn thread work hems. The drawn thread work hems make the corners into decorative squares; mitering is not required.

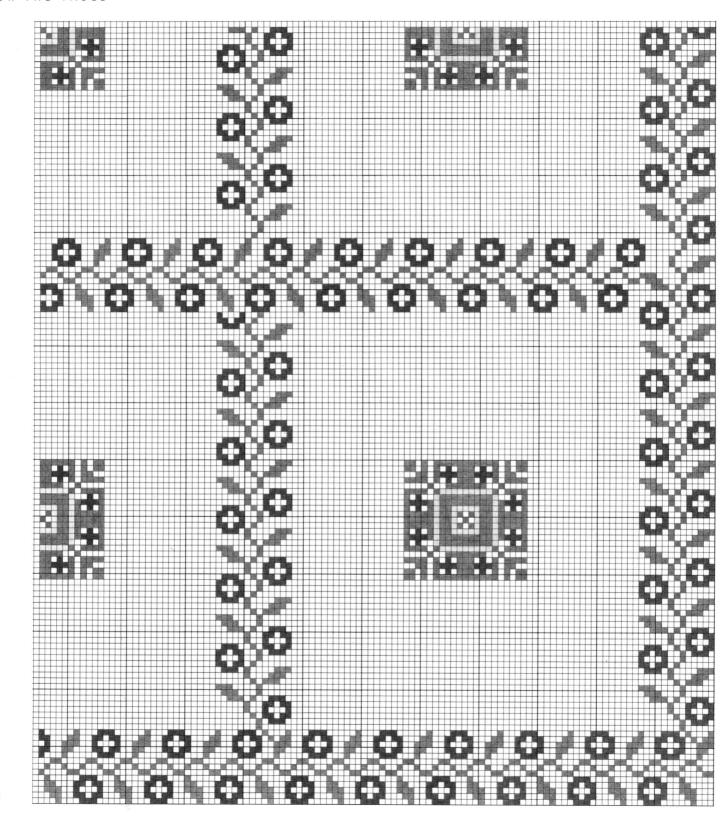

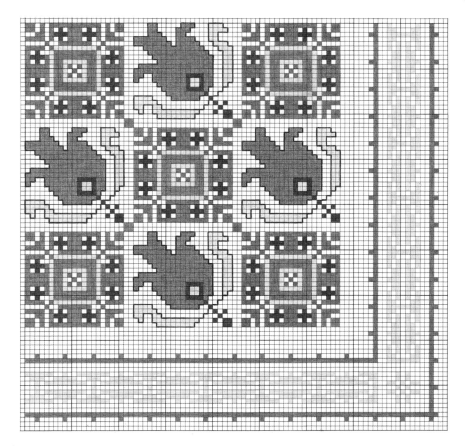

Thread colors

		Anchor	DMC
	cream	926	712
	blue	161	3760
	navy	164	824

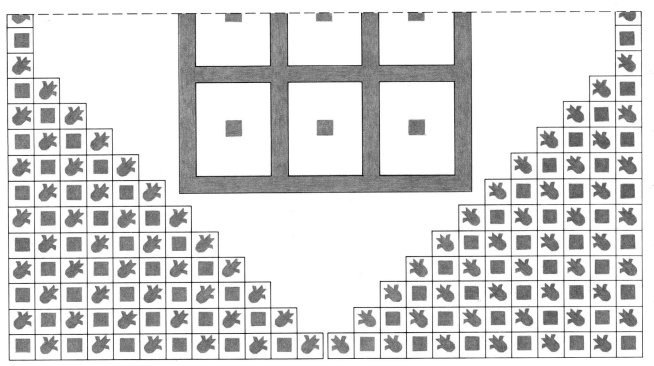

47

gingham table mats

Gingham is always popular and comes in a large range of bright and attractive colors. The checks can be used to provide a background ideal for plotting cross-stitch patterns. Depending on the size of the squares, one stitch can be worked over a single tiny square or, on a larger scale within a bigger square, four or five stitches can be used to make a symmetrical pattern.

Table mats made from gingham are a perfect project for the beginner. Choose a gingham with a similar pattern to the one in the pictures and remember to adapt the design to suit your fabric by drawing the medallion snowflake patterns (below) on graph paper. Consider the placement of motifs before cutting the fabric and make any necessary adjustments to the size of the mats at this stage. Charts for alternative medallion motifs are shown on pages 108–109.

About the table mats

Approximate finished size: 16" x 12¼"
(41 x 31cm), excluding trimming
Number of stitches per 1" (2.5cm): 12

You will need

For each mat:
17¼ " x 13½" (44 x 34cm) gingham
Backing fabric and interlining, cut to the
    same dimensions as the gingham
27" (70cm) trimming or braid
Crewel (embroidery) needle size 7
Cotton embroidery floss in the colors
    specified below
Use two strands of thread throughout

To work the design

1 Working from the chart, stitch the medallion motifs to fill the large gingham squares, working a single cross-stitch into each of the smaller squares on the fabric. Arrange the motifs onto the table mat to your own liking.

To finish

1 Along the short edges of both the gingham and the backing fabric, turn under and press ⅝" (1.5cm) to the wrong side. Cut off ⅝" (1.5cm) of the interlining fabric along both of the short edges. Place the interlining on the wrong side of the gingham, matching long edges, and folding the short side edge hems over the interlining to enclose the raw edges. Baste together the interlining and the gingham.

2 With right sides together, pin the backing fabric to the gingham along the long sides. Machine stitch the long sides, taking seam allowances of ⅝" (1.5cm), to make a tube. Turn the tube right side out and press the seams open, taking care not to flatten any cross-stitches.

3 Pin and baste the hemmed side edges together, then slipstitch. Stitch a length of trimming or braid in place over both side edges.

Thread colors

		Anchor	DMC
☐	yellow	278	472
■	blue	148	311
▨	rust	339	920

numbered napkin rings

Numbered napkin rings add a special touch to everyday dining and entertaining. House guests can be allotted their own personal napkin ring, for their sole use throughout the time of their stay. The cross-stitch numbers are worked over waste canvas, making the stitches easy to count. Quick to stitch, they add a stylish embellishment to classic moiré napkin rings. Choose a decorative button or bead to fasten the loop at the back and ring the changes by stitching a monogram, choosing the letter from one of the alphabets (see pages 98–101). You could make a set of these quite quickly as an unusual gift.

About the napkin rings

Approximate finished size: 8" x 2"
  (20 x 5cm), fastening to give a diameter
  of approximately 2" (5cm)
Number of stitches per 1" (2.5cm): 12

You will need

For each napkin ring:
20" (50cm) of 2" 5cm moiré
  grosgrain ribbon
Waste canvas, 12 threads per 1" (2.5cm)
Buckram interlining
Buttons or beads
Crewel (embroidery) needle size 7
Cotton embroidery floss in the colors
  specified below
Use two strands of floss throughout

To work the design

1 Fold the ribbon in half widthwise, marking the fold with basting stitches. With the right side of the ribbon facing, measure 6¼" (15.5cm) out from the fold toward one end of the ribbon. Mark this point with a line of basting stitches across the width of the ribbon to position the cross-stitch number.

2 Cut a piece of waste canvas 2½" (7cm) square, pin it centrally over the marked line, then baste it in place. Working from the chart, stitch a number through both the waste canvas and the ribbon. Alternatively, stitch a letter instead (see pages 98–101).

3 Once the stitching is complete, remove the waste canvas threads carefully (see page 17).

To finish

1 Measure 8⅜" (21cm) in each direction from the tacked, center fold line. Cut the piece of ribbon straight across the width at both ends.

2 With right sides together, fold one end of the ribbon lengthwise, so that the selvages meet. Pin and stitch along the raw edge, taking a seam allowance of ⅜" (1cm). Trim the corner close to the seam, press the seam open and turn right side out to make a pointed end. Finish the other end of the ribbon in the same way.

3 With wrong sides together, fold the ribbon in half so that the two pointed ends match exactly. Cut a shaped piece of buckram to fit the folded ribbon. Baste it in place, basting through all the layers together to keep them firm. Slipstitch all the way along the edges so as to encase the piece of buckram. Press carefully on the wrong side of the work.

4 Roll the napkin ring to give an overlap of approximately ¾" (2cm) and either stitch it in place or make a loop fastening. Sew on the button or bead fastening to complete the napkin ring.

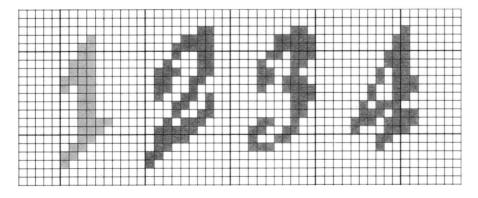

Thread colors

		Anchor	DMC
	lilac	870	3042
	gold	363	436
	pink	77	3350
	green	878	501

In the living room

Hand-worked pieces add an individual touch in the living room and these designs range from the traditional to the very contemporary.

The samplers and the pillow have been copied from original designs and adapted to fit any home, without losing any of their simplicity and charm. The director's chairs become stylish pieces of furniture with their covers embellished with a striking crown or heart motif. A soft woolen throw with a pretty cross-stitch border will disguise an old couch, or you could simply make the same ribbon border to edge a blanket to take with you on a picnic by the river, on a hot summer's day.

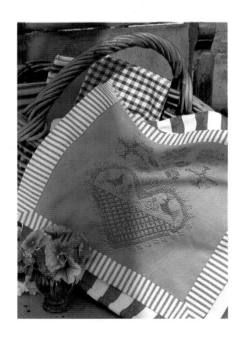

director's chair cover

Director's chairs have classic looks and simple lines that fit into almost any home or garden with perfect ease. They also have the practical advantage of folding almost flat, so they can be stored when not in use. The covers are put together inside out over each chair, making it possible to adapt them to fit any chair. The cross-stitch crown and heart motifs are worked in pearl threads and have a wonderful embossed texture; alternatively the motif can be made up on to a square of contrasting fabric, which can then be appliquéd to a finished chair cover.

About the chair cover

Cover fits a standard director's-style chair, with flat-topped wooden arms

Size of each completed motif:
Crown: 8¼" x10" (21 x 25cm);
Heart: 7" x 10½" (18 x 27cm)

Number of stitches per 1" (2.5cm): 11

You will need

3½yd (3.1m) strong cotton fabric, 48" (112cm) wide

Waste canvas, approximately15½" (40cm) square, 11 threads per 1" (2.5cm)

Crewel (embroidery) needle size 6

Pearl cotton in the colors specified on pages 56–57

Pattern paper or tailor's chalk

To cut out

1 Make a paper pattern for the cover using the dimensions of the chair, taken as described in the steps opposite. Each set of measurements makes a rectangular or square pattern piece (see diagram). Sketch it on paper first and then make a pattern to size before cutting out the fabric. Allow 3" (8cm) on each side for seams and hems this is a generous seam allowance which can be trimmed down later, after the cover has been made up. If you feel confident, you could draw directly on the wrong side of the fabric with tailor's chalk, adding a seam allowance as above. Where two pieces are needed (see step 7), remember to reverse the pattern if the shape is irregular.

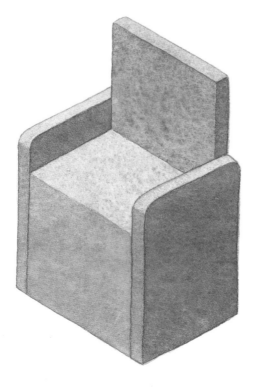

2 For the main piece (A), starting at floor level at the lower-back edge, measure up and over the chair, back down to the seat, then across the seat and down the front to the floor. This makes the long side of a rectangle. For the short side, measure the width of the seat (front edge and back), and the width of the chair, both at the top of the chair back and at floor level (front and back). Follow step 1 to make a pattern for piece A.

3 For the side panels (B), measure the dimensions along the floor (from front to back), along the top of the chair arm (front to back), and from the floor to the top of the chair arm at the front and at the back. Follow step 1 to make a pattern for piece B.

4 For the inside arms (C), measure the length of the chair arm, from where it meets the chair back to the front, the depth of the seat, and the distance (back and front) from the seat to the top of the arm. Follow step 1 to make a pattern for piece C.

5 For the arm gusset (D), start at the front of the chair and measure from the floor up to the front of the chair arm, along the top of the arm to the back of the chair, then down to the floor at the back. Measure the width of the chair arm. Follow step 1 to make a pattern for piece D.

6 For the side gussets (E), measure from the top of the arm at the back of the chair, to the top of the chair back, then measure the width of the wooden struts supporting the canvas chair back. Follow step 1 to make a pattern for piece E.

7 Pin the pattern pieces to the fabric, following the grain. Cut: 1 main piece (A), 2 side panels (B), 2 inside arms (C), 2 arm gussets (D), and 2 side gussets (E). Baste a line across the width of the main piece (A) to mark the top of the chair back and to use later for the positioning of the cross stitch motif (see page 56).

Key

A   Main piece (back, front)
B   Side panels
C   Inside arms
D   Arm gussets
E   Side gussets

A

B

C

D

E

To work the design

1 The motif is stitched on to the back of main piece (A) before the chair cover is made up. Position the motif by folding the back of piece A in half lengthwise, marking the fold with a line of basting stitches, following the grain of the fabric. Work another line of basting stitches running at right angles to the center fold line, parallel to and 9½" (24cm) from the basting line marking the top of the chair (see To cut out, step 7).

2 On the waste canvas, mark the central threads, running horizontally and vertically, then baste it in position on the right side of the fabric, matching the center markings to those on the fabric.

3 Work the cross-stitch motif over the waste canvas, following the charts and plotting the design from the center out toward the edges.

4 When the stitching is complete, remove the waste canvas one thread at a time.

5 Alternatively, the motif can be made up onto a square of fabric which you can then appliqué to a finished chair cover (see page 58).

Thread colors

		Anchor	DMC
	lilac	0939	793
	lightest blue	976	3325
	pale blue	0977	334
	mid blue	0978	322

Thread colors

		Anchor	DMC			Anchor	DMC
	pale gold	0887	422		gold	0888	420
	mid gold	0945	3046		lime	0278	472

To finish

1 Place the main piece (A), wrong side out, over the chair and pin side gussets (E), also wrong side out, in position on both sides. Make sure the back fits well over the chair but has some ease in it, so that when complete the seams are not strained and the cover is easily removed. Snip the seam allowance at the top corners on the main piece, to open around the top corners of the gusset. Remove the cover from the chair and sew the gussets in place, taking the seam allowance needed when pinned to fit.

2 Put the cover back on the chair, wrong side out, and pin the inside arm pieces (C) to the main piece (A), from the bottom of the side gussets, down to the seat, then along its outside edges. If they are irregular in shape, check each piece is in the correct place. Keep them in place along the top of the arm rests using tape. Snip the seam allowances and machine stitch the inside arms in place.

3 Put the cover back on the chair, wrong side out, and pin the arm gussets (D) in place up the front edges of the main piece (A) and inside arms (C), across the tops of the inside arms, along the bottoms of the side gussets (E), then down the side edges of the main piece at the back. Snip the seam allowances where necessary. Remove the cover from the chair and sew the arm gussets in place.

4 Put the cover back on the chair, wrong side out, and pin the side panels (B) in place along the edges of the arm gussets (D). Check that each piece is correctly placed. Snip seam allowances, remove from the chair and sew in the side panels.

5 Press open the seams, trim away excess bulky fabric, and neaten the edges.

6 Turn right side out and put in place over the chair. Turn under and pin a hem all around the bottom edge of the cover. Remove the cover from the chair and stitch the hem in place. Press to finish.

To appliqué the motif

If you prefer, you can buy a ready-made chair cover, as shown on page 53, on which to appliqué the motif. We used a contrasting fabric for backing the chair.

1 Cut a 11" (28cm) square of fabric. Position the design following the instructions on page 16.

2 Work the motif over the waste canvas, following the chart on page 56 plotting the design from the center out toward the edges. Carefully remove the waste canvas to complete (see page 17). Turn a small single hem and press.

3 For the contrasting border, measure and cut four strips of fabric, 4" (10cm) wide by the length of the hemmed square, plus an extra 4" (10cm) for mitering the corners. Fold the pieces in half along the width, miter the corners (see page 18) and sew onto the square.

4 Appliqué the finished square to the back of a finished chair cover.

blue panel curtains

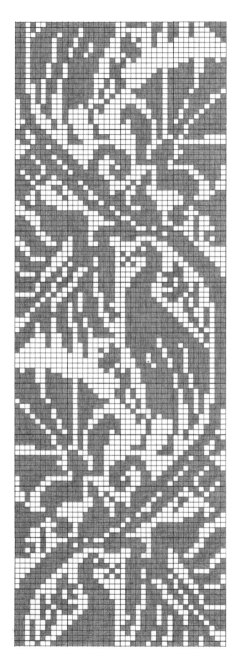

Embroidered panels add a lavish finishing touch to curtains in the living room. Cross-stitch designs, worked in bands that run horizontally, can be used to make borders or to edge a heading on simple country curtains. The basic lines of a ticking stripe suit this style of decoration particularly well; the top, in contrasting ticking, forms an unusual soft, bunched heading when the curtains are drawn back.

The panels are worked separately and are then stitched on the curtains before they are finished. This allows plenty of scope for different fabric combinations to coordinate with the patterned panels. Alternatively, for a plainer effect, the panel design can be worked directly onto a wide linen fabric to form the main body of the curtains.

About the curtains

Approximate finished size of each curtain:
36" (90cm) long x 47" (120cm) wide
Size of one repeat pattern: 9½" x 3" (24 x 8cm)
Number of stitches per 1" (2.5cm): 12/13
Work stitches over two threads at a time when using fabric with double the thread count

Note

As a general guide, this style of curtain needs to be 1½–2 times the width of the window. Curtains made to the size given above will suit a window 47"–63" (120-160cm) wide by 36" (90cm) long. Adapt the measurements to the required size.

You will need

For a pair of curtains:
½yd (30cm) even-weave linen,55" (140cm) wide, 25 threads per 1" (2.5cm)
2½yd (2.2m) ticking fabric, 55" (140cm) wide
1¼yd (1m) contrasting fabric, 55" (140cm) wide (for the heading flap)
2¾yd (2.5m) of standard, gathered curtain tape, 1¼" (3cm) wide
4 curtain weights
Tapestry needle size 24
Cotton embroidery floss in the color below
Use two strands of thread throughout

To work the design

1 Fold the linen in half lengthwise and cut along the fold, following the grain of the fabric, to make two strips. Fold one of the strips in half again lengthwise and mark the fold line with pins. Work a row of basting stitches, following the grain of the fabric, to mark the center line. Mark the second strip in the same way.
2 Beginning 1¼" (3cm) up from one end of one of the strips, begin to plot out the design, following the chart and placing the pattern centrally on the linen. Continue to work the panel until the required length has been completed. Work the second panel in the same way.

To finish

1 Cut the main fabric to make two equal sized pieces to the required length, allowing an extra 6" (16cm) at the bottom for the hem and 1¼" (3cm) at the top. Fold over a double hem, turning under 3" (8cm) twice. Press and baste. Turn 3½" (9cm) to the wrong side on each side edge and catch the edges down with large herringbone stitches, ending 7" (18cm) above each bottom corner. Miter the hem at each bottom corner and sew a curtain weight inside, then complete the herringbone stitching. Slipstitch the bottom hem in place.
2 For each panel, trim the fabric to within ⅜" (1cm) of the stitching, then turn the edges to the wrong side, to the edge of the stitching, and baste. Position the panels on the curtain so the bottom edges of the panels are level with the hemline and there is a 4" (10cm) border of fabric along the inside edges, where the curtains will meet when drawn. Slipstitch the panels in place.
3 Cut two pieces of fabric, each measuring 55" x 18½" (140 x 46cm), for the heading flaps. Turn under 3½" (9cm) to

Thread color

	Anchor	DMC
■ blue	169	806

the wrong side on each of the short side edges. Hold in place with neat rows of herringbone stitches.

4 With right sides together, pin one long edge of a heading flap along the top edge of a curtain piece, so that the edge of the heading is ⅝" (1.5cm) down from the top edge of the curtain. Stitch together, taking the seam allowance from the top edge of the heading. Turn the heading to the right side and press the seam flat, up toward the heading.

5 Fold under ⅝" (1.5cm) to the wrong side along the other long edge of the heading. Press and baste. Fold the heading in half lengthwise so that the turned edge meets the sewing line on the back of the curtain. Slipstitch in place.

6 With the heading flat, pin curtain tape to the back of the curtain so that the bottom edge runs slightly below the heading stitching line. Cut the tape to fit, turning under the ends to neaten them. Stitch in place through all thicknesses of fabric.

strawberry ribbon throw

The throw pictured here has been cleverly used to cover up an old couch, but it could be used to equal advantage over a bed, or even as a blanket in its own right. The border is cross stitched onto a pretty velvet ribbon which trims a soft, wool challis blanket. It is cross stitched here with a delicate strawberry pattern, but you can choose another design from a selection of alternatives which includes hearts, florals and cherries, these are featured on pages 106 and 107.

About the throw

Approximate finished size: 77½" x 53"
   (197 x 135cm)
Number of stitches per 1" (2.5cm): 14

You will need

8yd (7.25m) ribbon, at least 1½" (4cm)
   wide (We used cotton velvet for this
   throw. If you choose another type of
   ribbon make sure that it is firm)
2¼ yd (2m) fine woven wool fabric,
   2¼ yd (138cm) wide (we used 100 per
   cent wool challis)
Waste canvas, 14 threads per 1" (2.5cm)
Crewel (embroidery) needle size 7 or 8
Cotton embroidery floss in the colors
   specified below.
Use two strands of floss throughout

To work the design

1 Following the threads, cut the waste canvas into strips. These should measure at least 1½" (4cm) wide, each side than the ribbon.
2 Measure the ribbon carefully along the fabric, allowing approximately 2" (5cm) extra at the corners for the hem and overlap. Alternatively, if you prefer to miter (see page 18), measure and cut the ribbon into four lengths.
3 Leaving approximately 2" (5cm) free

for each corner, baste the waste canvas in place onto the first length of ribbon, checking that its threads are in line with the ribbon edges. You may find it easier to work with only a small piece of waste canvas each time.
4 Work the motifs from the chart, counting the threads on the canvas and allowing a space of three stitches between each motif. For mitered corners, leave an unstitched area of ribbon to turn under so that only whole motifs are visible.
5 Carefully remove the waste canvas one thread at a time.
6 Continue to work along the remaining lengths of ribbon in the same way.

To finish

1 Turn under the selvages along both sides of the length of fabric and carefully hem in place. Carefully baste and lightly press the two remaining sides and then work a small double hem.
2 Pin, then baste the ribbon to the right side of the fabric, overlapping or mitering the corners neatly.
3 Hand sew or machine stitch the ribbon in place along all four edges of the throw. Remove the basting. Press lightly on the wrong side of the fabric, taking care not to flatten the stitching.

Thread colors

		Anchor	DMC
	crimson	19	347
	scarlet	46	666
	yellow	307	783
	dark green	268	3345
	green	266	3347
	cream	885	3047
	ecru	372	738
	rust	347	402
	brown	349	301
	green	845	3011
	chartreuse	907	832
	straw	956	677

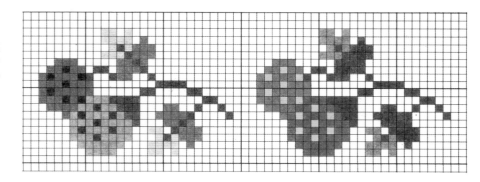

church sampler

Samplers play a significant part of the history of embroidery. Their stitched patterns have timeless charm, and the traditional motifs used to embellish them have particular character – the essence of birds, trees, houses, and people are often captured in just a few carefully placed stitches.

Originally, samplers were used to provide a record of the different kinds of stitches and patterns for both professional and amateur needleworkers. Examples of these exist from the early sixteenth century. During the eighteenth and nineteenth centuries, they were more often used as a teaching exercise; most young girls were expected to work at least one sampler over the course of their education, usually including alphabets and numerals as part of the design. Toward the end of the nineteenth century samplers became appreciated much more for purely aesthetic reasons.

The next three projects involve samplers of quite different types, reflecting their development from the early days. By using the charts on pages 98–101 you can incorporate references to your own family in the samplers, to make exquisite works of art both to decorate your home and to become treasured heirlooms.

About the sampler

Approximate finished size: 13½" x 13"
  (34 x 33cm), excluding frame
Number of stitches per 1" (2.5cm): 18
Work stitches over two threads at a time
  for the design, except the lettering,
  see below

You will need

29" (73cm) even-weave linen, 29½"
  (74cm) wide, 36 threads per 1"
  (2.5cm)
Tapestry needle size 26
Cotton embroidery floss in the colors
  specified on pages 66–69
Use two strands of floss throughout

To work the design

1 Decide what lettering you would like to include. The stitches making the lettering on the original sampler were half the size of those of the rest of the sampler (although the letters can be up to eight stitches high, they are equal to the height of only four stitches of the rest of the design). To achieve this, work over one thread for the lettering, instead of two. Using the alphabets given on pages 98–101, draft the lettering on to graph paper. What you choose is a matter of personal preference; you can either include references to your own family or favorite pets in the sampler; or you can work a simple alphabet. Work out whether the lettering will look best over one or two lines. Bear in mind that each square on the chart is equal to two (half-size) lettering stitches.

2 Mark the position of the border with pins, on the fabric. Taking a side at a time, make one row of basting stitches approximately 8½" (22cm) from one long edge, then make another row, running parallel to the first, but 17 stitches (34 threads) in from it.

3 Following the chart, stitch the outside border line (pale green) within the basting lines until one corner is reached. Count and stitch the diagonal corner; then repeat in the same way, making the two basting lines for the next side and stitch to the next corner. The dark green inside line of the border may be stitched either at this stage or later, whichever you prefer.

4 Once the border is completed, the other elements are easier to position. Begin with the church. Position its base by counting 40 stitches from the right border, 42 stitches from the left border and 3 stitches up from the lower border.

5 Next, stitch the lettering, (see step 1) in the space below the church. The flowers, trees, and so on are now easier to place in relation to the border and church.

6 Trim the fabric, leaving a large enough border all around for mounting and framing the sampler (see page 19).

Thread colors

		Anchor	DMC			Anchor	DMC
	pink	1024	107		pale gold	887	422
	dark brown	358	433		ecru	390	3033
	light brown	375	420		flesh	880	951
	gold	373	3045		dark green	217	319

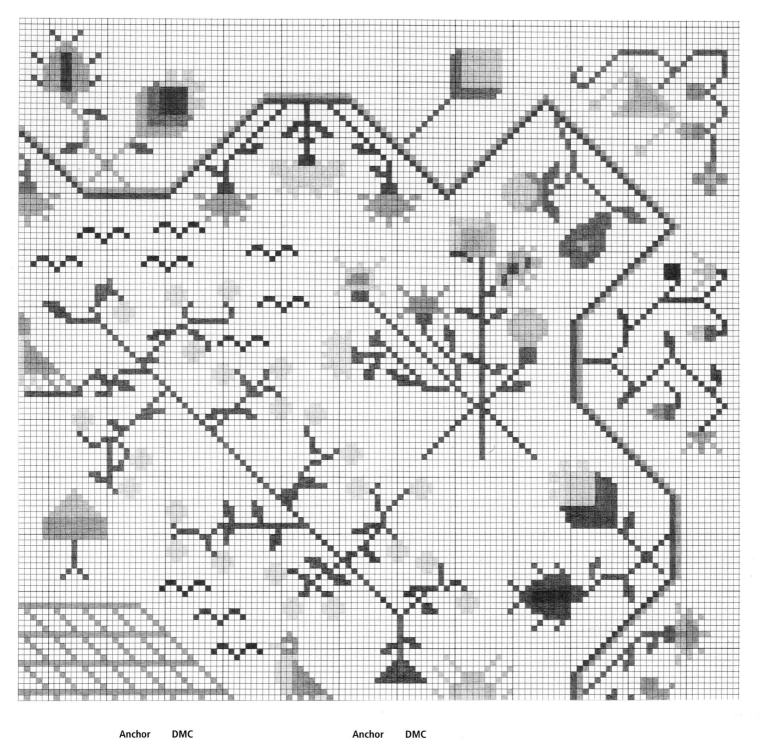

		Anchor	DMC			Anchor	DMC
	sage	860	3363		black	403	310
	leaf green	843	3012				
	pale green	854	3013				
	blue	168	807				

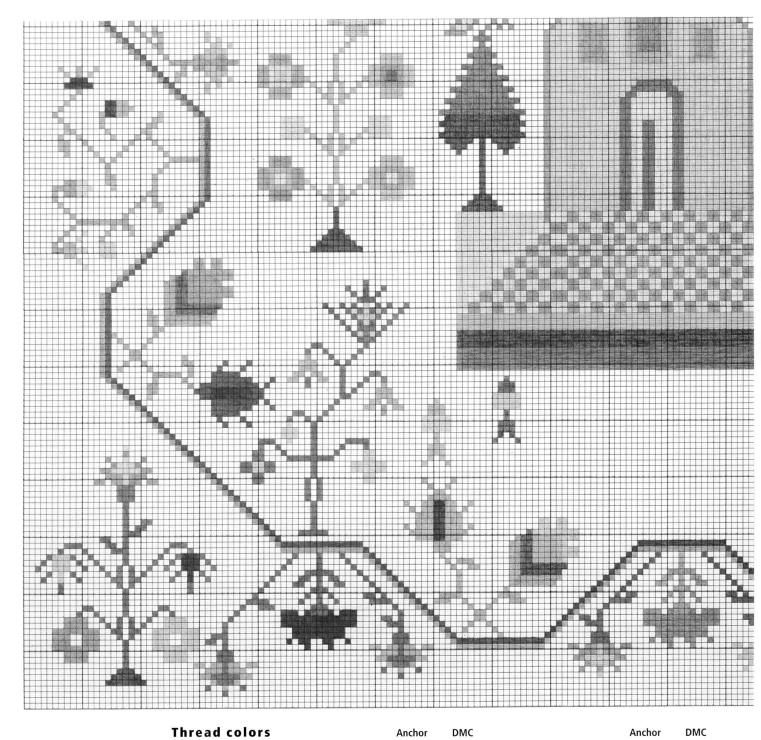

Thread colors

	Anchor	DMC			Anchor	DMC
pink	1024	107		pale gold	887	422
dark brown	358	433		ecru	390	3033
light brown	375	420		flesh	880	951
gold	373	3045		dark green	217	319

	Anchor	DMC			Anchor	DMC
sage	860	3363	black	403	310
leaf-green	843	3012			
pale-green	854	3013			
blue	168	807			

school sampler

Old school samplers provide a wealth of inspiration for motifs and border designs, many of them looking just as fresh now as when they were originally worked. This Annan School sampler, stitched by Barbara Weall in 1870, features symmetrically arranged motifs of flowers and fruit baskets with a remarkably contemporary feel. Set out in three bold bands across the sampler, the urns and pots, filled with stylized blooms, capture the atmosphere of a formal garden. Initials of family members have been incorporated into the alphabet and a border of numerals has been stitched across the top.

It is easier to work your own family tree into a similar design, but if making this design seems overly ambitious, a scaled-down version, made up of a few pots of flowers contained within a border, would look just as special.

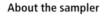

About the sampler

Approximate finished size: 24¾" x 19½"
 (63 x 49.5cm), excluding frame
Number of stitches per 1" (2.5cm): 14
Work stitches over two threads at a time
 when using fabric with double the
 thread count

You will need

35½" (89.5cm) even-weave linen,
 40¾" (103cm) wide, 28 threads per
 1" (2.5cm)
Tapestry needle size 24
Either cotton floss, using two strands,
 or Paternayan Persian yarn, using
 one strand. The original piece was
 worked in wool on linen canvas, giving
 a textured, raised effect. In the charts
 on pages 72–75, colors are given for
 embroidery floss, which will produce a
 less ridged, more refined result.

To work the design

1 Begin by deciding on the lettering to include in the sampler. Using the charted alphabet (see page 72), draft the letters on graph paper and arrange them over one or two lines. Center the lettering for ease of positioning (see step 5).

2 Start by stitching the inside line of the border in dark green. Mark 9½" (24cm) in from one short edge and work a straight horizontal line of 308 stitches along one long side, starting 9½" (24cm) in from the edge. This forms the base of the inside of the border.

3 Next work the short edges over 232

stitches, use the first and last stitches of the base row just worked as a guide for the bottom corners.

4 Work the top row in the same way. Counting down from the top row, work the three straight lines of the top lettering, then the three remaining horizontal lines running across the sampler.

5 Once these guide lines are in place it is

up to you to decide which order you will work in.

It is helpful to baste a line down the center of the fabric. This is useful as a guide to work the lettering, border, school and flower motifs.

6 Trim the fabric, leaving a large enough border all the way around for mounting and framing the sampler (see page 19).

71

Thread colors

		Anchor	DMC			Anchor	DMC
	red	47	304		sage	844	3012
	yellow	280	581		turquoise	779	926
	bottle	879	500		blue	921	931

		Anchor	DMC			Anchor	DMC
	gray	399	318		light brown	351	400
	black	403	310		beige	853	613
	brown	381	938		soft gray	388	3782

Thread colors

		Anchor	DMC			Anchor	DMC
	red	47	304		sage	844	3012
	yellow	280	581		turquoise	779	926
	bottle	879	500		blue	921	931

		Anchor	DMC			Anchor	DMC
	gray	399	318		light brown	351	400
	black	403	310		beige	853	613
	brown	381	938		soft gray	388	3782

sampler pillow

A sampler pillow is a practical way to show off your handiwork, at the same time adding a traditional element to a living room. Motifs of naturalistic subjects, such as animals, birds, trees, and people, became especially popular during the nineteenth century when the purely decorative aspect of samplers began to be recognized. This sampler pillow design includes a menagerie of animals and a simple twining border embellished with flowers, orchard fruits, and garden architecture. Incorporate motifs of family pets or favorite flowers to make it your own secret garden.

About the pillow

Approximate finished size: 18" (45cm) square

Number of stitches per 1" (2.5cm) 14

Work stitches over two threads at a time when using fabric with double the thread count

You will need

31" x 27" (78 x 68cm) Irish linen, 28 threads per 1" (2.5cm)

The fabric should be "tea dyed" (see page 19)

2 pieces of matching fabric, 19¼" (48cm), for the pillow back

Pillow form, 18" (46cm) square approximately

2yd (2m) cording or fringe (optional)

Tapestry needle size 24

Anchor or DMC cotton floss in the colors on page 78

Use two strands of floss throughout

The pillow photographed was made using Anchor threads, so to achieve an exact likeness you should use the same.

To work the design

1 Run two rows of basting stitches – one lengthwise, one widthwise – through the center of the fabric. Now run a line of basting stitches 8" (20cm) in from the outer edge, all around the fabric, representing the size of the finished pillow.

2 Stitch the border outline working from the chart, beginning at the center of one side and working eight stitches in from the basting line.

3 Work the alphabet, starting at the center and counting down from the border.

4 Work the ivy leaf pattern under the alphabet in the same way.

5 Once the border and the basting lines are in place, you can use them as a guide when placing the other motifs, which you are free to stitch in any order.

To cut out

Before cutting or making any adjustments, check the measurements of the stitched piece carefully. Measuring an even border of plain fabric all around the stitched area, cut the embroidered piece to 19¼" x 12¾" (48 x 32 cm); this includes a seam allowance on every side of ⅝" (1.5cm).

To finish

1 Fold under the ⅝" (1.5cm) seam allowance along lower and upper edges of the embroidered piece and press.

2 Pin the embroidery on to the right side of one piece of fabric, placing it centrally. Leave 3¾" (9.5cm) of the main fabric visible at the top and the bottom.

3 Using soft embroidery cotton, blanket stitch the embroidered piece to the main fabric along upper and lower edges.

4 If you decide to use cording or fringe, first baste it along the right side of the pillow piece, close to the sewing line. Make sure that the part of the fringe to be seen on the finished pillow lies to the inside of the seam line. Carefully ease or snip the trimming around corners.

5 With right sides together, baste, then machine stitch all around the pillow, leaving a gap large enough in one side to insert the pillow form. Carefully remove the basting stitches.

6 Turn the pillow right side out and press the edges carefully, taking care not to flatten the piping or fringing if used.

7 Insert the pillow form.

8 Close the opening with slipstitch.

Thread colors

		Anchor	DMC
	yellow	874	834
	gold	901	680
	sienna	375	420
	green	844	3012
	dark green	263	3362
	blue	977	334
	gray	847	3072
	pink	1027	3722
	rust	884	400
	brown	358	433
	dark brown	382	3371

Household items

This final section of cross-stitch projects for the home includes a wealth of decorative ideas. Shelf edgings were once a common feature over the mantle piece in both country cottages and town houses; in this chapter, teacup designs are used to enhance a shelf edging and a tea cozy.

Borders are always popular, and the one that is used here to decorate the huck towel could be exchanged for another of the other designs illustrated on pages 106–107, in fact you could make a set of towels, stitching a different pattern along each border. The three linen bags show a different use for cross-stitch. Appliqué motifs are attached to the bags with freehand cross-stitches, that are also used to embellish the appliqué designs.

shelf edging

This pretty teacup edging for a shelf or mantle piece is easy to stitch once the motifs are positioned. Work them in one of the color schemes shown on the charts here or on page 84; alternatively use your own scheme to match the decorations at home. This design would complement a collection of china which you want to show to its best advantage.

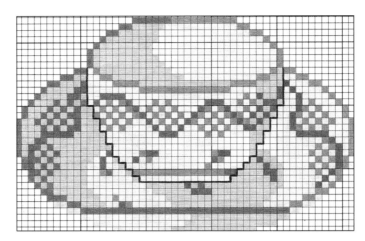

Thread colors

		Anchor	DMC
☐	cream	926	822
	gray	397	762
	china blue	978	322
	royal blue	979	312
	navy	922	930

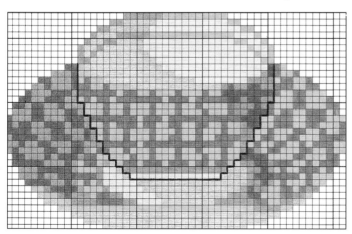

Thread colors

		Anchor	DMC
☐	cream	885	3047
	ecru	899	869
	yellow	307	783
	orange	337	922
	rust	339	920
	brown	341	918

About the shelf edging

Depth: 5½" (14cm)
Size of each motif: 4¾" wide x 2¾" high (12cm x 7cm)
Space between each motif: 1¼" (3cm) approximately
Number of stitches per 1" (2.5cm): 11

You will need

One piece natural Aida, 10⅝" (27cm) deep by the required length, 11 threads per 1" (2.5cm). (Depth includes 4½" (11.5cm) to attach to top of shelf, adjustable if necessary)
Calico for lining, 6⅛" (15.5cm) deep by required length
Ribbon trim (optional), same length as shelf
Tapestry needle size 24
Cotton embroidery floss in the colors specified here
Use two strands of thread throughout

To work the design

1 First work out the spacing of the motifs. In the sample shown here, the motifs are 52 stitches wide with a space of 14 stitches between them therefore, each motif requires a total space of 66 stitches. Use these figures to calculate how many motifs will fit on your shelf edging; the size of the motif will remain constant (52 stitches), so adjust the size of the space as necessary.
2 Run vertical basting lines, approximately 5½" (14cm) long, from the lower edge of the fabric. Position them at 66-stitch intervals (adjust for your spacing) to indicate the center of each motif.
3 Position the bottom row of motifs 1¾" (4.5cm) up from lower edge of the fabric, matching the center of the chart to the basting lines.
4 Stitch the motifs following the charts.
5 Remove the basting stitches.

To finish

1 With right sides together and taking a ⅝" (1.5cm) seam allowance, baste, then sew the calico lining to the bottom edge of the stitched fabric. Turn right side out and press the double thickness.

2 Pin the ribbon trimming to the shelf edging through all the layers, 5" (13cm) up from the lower edge, so that it runs along the shelf edge.

3 Baste and stitch the ribbon and lining. Remove the basting.

4 Attach the edging to the shelf top with the spare fabric, using tacks or glue.

tea cozy

Worked in the same attractive design as this shelf edging, the tea cozy has a thick lining for good insulation which will help to keep your tea piping hot! Stitch the tea using the chart below or alternatively, choose the same color scheme as the shelf edging, the two make a charming, complementary pair; and the tea cozy will happily grace any kitchen table for many years to come.

About the tea cozy

Approximate finished size: 15¼" wide x 10¼" high (39 x 26cm)
Size of each motif 4⅝" x 3" (12 x 7.5cm)
Space between each motif: 1½" (3cm)
Number of stitches per 1" (2.5cm): 11

You will need

16½" x 6¼" (42 x 15.5cm) natural Aida, 11 stitches per 1" (2.5cm
18" (30cm) of 43" (110cm) wide cotton fabric (we used cotton herringbone in ecru)
60cm (1yd) of 110cm (43in) wide cotton lining fabric
2 pieces wadding, 16½" x 11½in" (42 x 29cm)
Tissue paper
Tapestry needle size 24
Cotton embroidery floss in the colors specified left.
Use two strands of floss throughout

To work the design

1 Run two vertical lines of basting stitches about 5" (13cm) in from the two short edges of the Aida, indicating the centers of the two motifs.

2 Placing the bottom row of motifs 1½" (4cm) up from the lower edge of the fabric, match the center of the chart to the basting lines and stitch the motifs, working from the chart.

3 Remove the basting stitches.

To finish

1 Make a tissue paper template of the tea cozy. Begin with a rectangle measuring 16½" x 11½" (42 x 29cm). Draw, then cut out, a curve on one side. Fold the tissue paper in half and cut the other side to match.

2 Cut out two pieces of both the cotton fabric and the wadding. Cut out four pieces of lining fabric in the same way .

3 Measure and fold under a ⅝" (1.5cm) seam along the upper edge of the embroidered trimming. Press the seam.

4 With right sides facing, lay the embroidered trimming over one piece of fabric so that the lower edges line up. Baste, then slipstitch the upper edge of the trimming to the fabric.

5 With right sides together, baste, then sew a ⅝" (1.5cm) seam around the curved edge of the fabric pieces. Repeat with both pairs of lining pieces, taking a ¾" (2cm) seam allowance. Do not stitch the lower edge of either lining. Snip the curves where necessary, press and remove the basting.

6 Turn one of the linings right side out and put the second one inside it. Push the two pieces of wadding in between. Turn under the bottom edges of both linings and hand sew together. Secure the wadding with a few quilting stitches.

7 Fold under and press a turning of ⅝" (1.5cm) along the lower edges of the cozy cover. Insert the inner piece and slipstitch to the tea cozy cover along the lower edge.

Thread colors

		Anchor	DMC
☐	cream	885	3047
	dark cream	880	951
	yellow	891	676
	gold	313	977
	pale pink	75	3354
	dark pink	77	3350
	pale green	876	503
	dark green	878	501

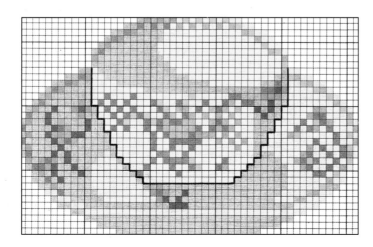

huck towel

Linen is robust, hardwearing and highly absorbent, making it an ideal fabric for hand and bath towels. Huck weave linen is traditionally used for this purpose and has a classic elegance that is hard to match.

Old huck towels can be found in junk shops, often in good condition, which testifies to the enduring qualities of linen. Embellish them with geometric, floral, or leafy borders chosen from the charts on pages 106–107. The regular nubs, which form the texture of this fabric, are easy to use as a guide for working cross stitch patterns.

About the towel

Approximate finished size: 24" x 44"
 (61 x 112cm)
Number of stitches per 1" (2.5cm): 13

You will need

35" (88cm) huck linen, 24"
 (61cm) wide,
or an old huck towel
1½yd (1.3m) lace or openwork edging,
 5" (13cm) deep
Crewel (embroidery) needle size 6 or 7
Cotton embroidery floss in the colors
 below
Use two strands of floss throughout

To work the design

Depending on the weave of the fabric, the number of threads per 1" (2.5cm) may vary, thus altering the scale of the border, so before beginning it will be necessary to calculate how many stitches should be worked to the inch.
1 Fold the linen in half lengthwise and mark the center fold line with a row of basting stitches, following the grain of the fabric indicated by the nubby textured weave.

2 Measure 1" (2.5cm) in from the short edge of the fabric and use pins to mark a line the length of the short edge, then make a row of basting stitches, following the grain of the fabric. This line marks the bottom edge of the border.
3 Stitch the border, plotting the design from the center of the chart and the basted central line on the fabric, working out toward the long edges.
4 Work the other end of the cloth in the same way if required.
5 Remove the basting stitches.

To finish

1 Along both short ends of the fabric, turn under ¼" (5mm) twice to the wrong side. Slipstitch in place. If possible leave the long edges as selvages, however if the fabric has been cut to size it will be necessary to turn under small double hems in the same way.
2 Cut a length of openwork or lace edging to fit both short ends of the hemmed fabric. Finish the side edges with tiny hems. Press lightly.
3 Pin and baste the edging to the fabric and slipstitch in place. Press to complete.

Thread colors

		Anchor	DMC
■	blue	848	927
▨	pink	838	3064

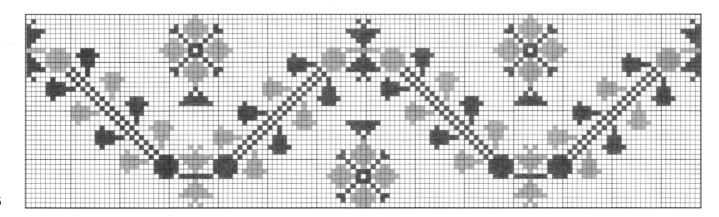

three linen bags

Unusual bags made from scraps of colorful fabric provide useful and attractive storage places for keeping gym or ballet shoes tidy, or for hiding dirty clothing while it awaits wash day. Ticking stripes and checkered fabrics, mixed together for the appliqué patches, give these laundry bags a folk art appeal. Freehand cross-stitches secure the patches in place and any uneven stitching adds to their charm, making these perfect projects for anyone whose stitching lacks precision. Tiny pearl and linen buttons can be used for extra decoration, picking up the detail of the garments depicted in the motifs. If the ticking colors look too new, try using the wrong side of the fabric; it often has a more faded appearance which is especially appealing for this style of project.

16½" (31 x 42cm).

2 For the drawstring channel, cut two strips of contrasting fabric, each 12¼" x 3¼" (31 x 10cm).

To stitch together

1 With right sides facing, pin and baste the back and front together along the sides and bottom edges. Stitch, then turn right side out and press.

2 With right sides facing, stitch the drawstring channel strips together along a short edge and press the seam flat. Turn under ⅝" (1.5cm) to the wrong side on both remaining short edges and stitch. Turn in the same amount along both long edges, press and baste.

3 Fold the strip in half lengthwise and place over the raw edges of the top of the bag encasing it; the open ends of the strip meet at a side seam. Baste, then work a row of cross-stitches along the edge of the strip on the outside. Slipstitch the strip to the inside and join the ends.

4 Thread the grosgrain ribbon through the channel to make a loop and pin the ends together. Cut two matching triangles from a scrap of fabric. Turn under the edges and slipstitch them together, feed the ends of the drawstring into the triangle before stitching up the third side.

Shoe bag

About the bag
Approximate finished size of bag:
    11½" x 18½" (29 x 41cm)
Seam allowances are ⅝" (1.5cm)

You will need
½yd (50cm) ticking fabric x 56" (142cm)
¼yd (10cm) contrasting fabric, 36"
    (90cm) wide, for drawstring channel
1¼yd (1.2m) grosgrain ribbon, (¾")
    17mm wide, for drawstring
Assorted fabric scraps
Tracing paper
Crewel (embroidery) needle size 6 or 7
Pearl cotton floss in assorted colors

To cut out
1 For the front and back of the bag, cut two rectangles of ticking, each 12¼" x

To work the design

1 Trace the shoe motifs from the outlines below to make pattern pieces, then cut the two shoes from a contrasting fabric. Cut two pieces from another fabric to make the shapes for inside the shoes. Turn under ¼" (5mm) around all the pieces, snipping curves where necessary. Baste around the edges, then press.

2 Position, pin and baste the shoe shapes to the bag, then position and baste the shapes for inside the shoes. Work evenly spaced cross-stitches around the edges of the shapes to secure them in place.

3 Use tiny cross-stitches to hold down lengths of thread, representing the flaps for the laces and the place where the shoe upper meets the sole. Add more cross-stitches at random to decorate the shoes to your own taste.

4 Using two strands of thread, stitch through the fabric to make long loops similar to shoe laces. Tie them in a bow, finishing off the ends with small knots. Work freehand cross-stitches in a random arrangement around the shoes or you can follow the illustration if you prefer.

5 Remove basting to complete.

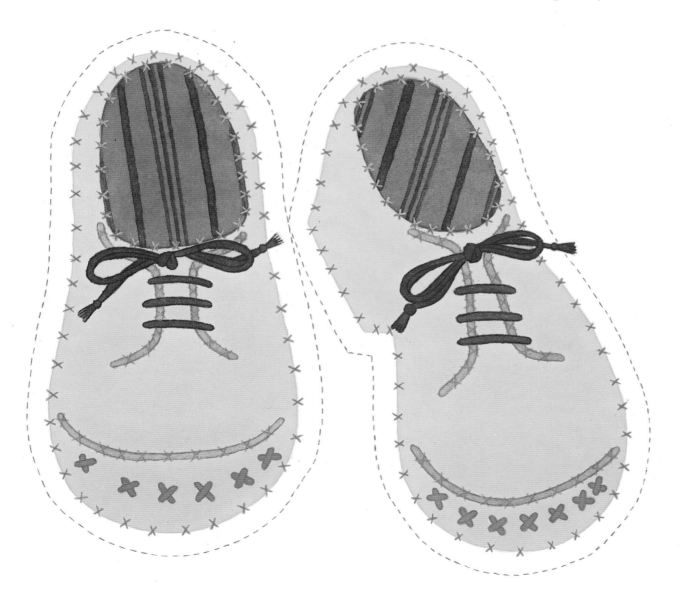

Lingerie bag

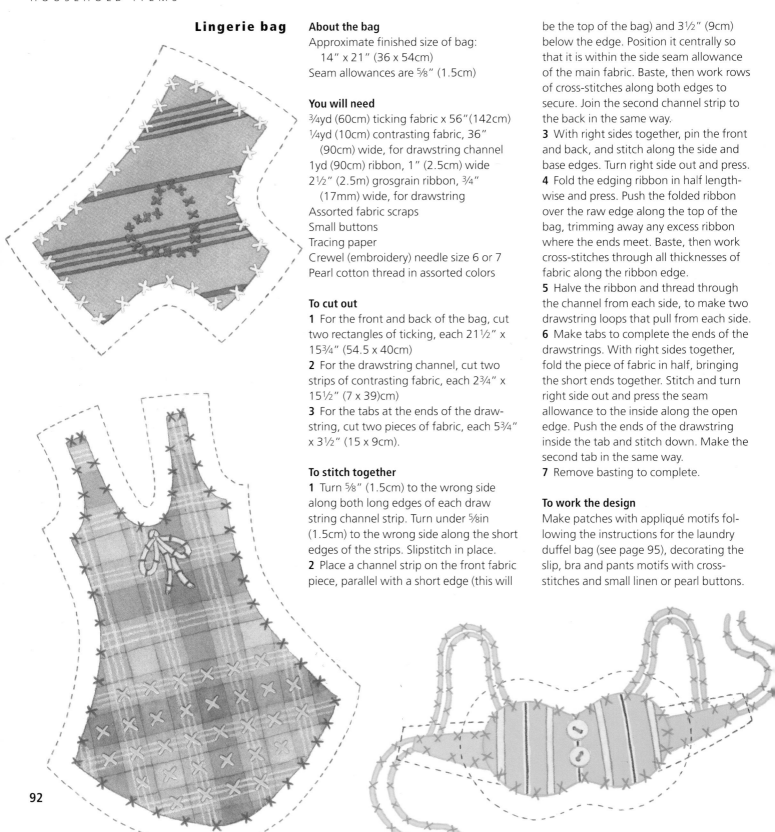

About the bag

Approximate finished size of bag:
   14" x 21" (36 x 54cm)
Seam allowances are ⅝" (1.5cm)

You will need

¾yd (60cm) ticking fabric x 56"(142cm)
¼yd (10cm) contrasting fabric, 36"
   (90cm) wide, for drawstring channel
1yd (90cm) ribbon, 1" (2.5cm) wide
2½" (2.5m) grosgrain ribbon, ¾"
   (17mm) wide, for drawstring
Assorted fabric scraps
Small buttons
Tracing paper
Crewel (embroidery) needle size 6 or 7
Pearl cotton thread in assorted colors

To cut out

1 For the front and back of the bag, cut two rectangles of ticking, each 21½" x 15¾" (54.5 x 40cm)
2 For the drawstring channel, cut two strips of contrasting fabric, each 2¾" x 15½" (7 x 39)cm)
3 For the tabs at the ends of the drawstring, cut two pieces of fabric, each 5¾" x 3½" (15 x 9cm).

To stitch together

1 Turn ⅝" (1.5cm) to the wrong side along both long edges of each draw string channel strip. Turn under ⅝in (1.5cm) to the wrong side along the short edges of the strips. Slipstitch in place.
2 Place a channel strip on the front fabric piece, parallel with a short edge (this will be the top of the bag) and 3½" (9cm) below the edge. Position it centrally so that it is within the side seam allowance of the main fabric. Baste, then work rows of cross-stitches along both edges to secure. Join the second channel strip to the back in the same way.
3 With right sides together, pin the front and back, and stitch along the side and base edges. Turn right side out and press.
4 Fold the edging ribbon in half lengthwise and press. Push the folded ribbon over the raw edge along the top of the bag, trimming away any excess ribbon where the ends meet. Baste, then work cross-stitches through all thicknesses of fabric along the ribbon edge.
5 Halve the ribbon and thread through the channel from each side, to make two drawstring loops that pull from each side.
6 Make tabs to complete the ends of the drawstrings. With right sides together, fold the piece of fabric in half, bringing the short ends together. Stitch and turn right side out and press the seam allowance to the inside along the open edge. Push the ends of the drawstring inside the tab and stitch down. Make the second tab in the same way.
7 Remove basting to complete.

To work the design

Make patches with appliqué motifs following the instructions for the laundry duffel bag (see page 95), decorating the slip, bra and pants motifs with cross-stitches and small linen or pearl buttons.

Laundry duffel bag

About the bag

Approximate finished size of bag:
    27" high x 35½"
    diameter (69 x 90cm)
Seam allowances are ⅝" (1.5cm)

You will need

1¼yd (1.1m) ticking fabric, 56"
    142cm wide
¼yd (20cm) calico, 36" (90cm) wide
Assorted fabric scraps
Small buttons
Tracing paper
Crewel (embroidery) needle size 6 or 7
Pearl cotton floss in assorted colors

To cut out

1 Cut a ticking rectangle , 47¼" x 26¾"

(120 x 68cm), for the main piece.

2 Cut a circle of ticking, 15¼" (39cm) in diameter, for the base.

3 For the drawstring, cut two strips of calico, each 3¼" x 30" (8 x 76cm).

4 For the drawstring tabs, cut 14 rectangles from the fabric scraps as follows: two pieces 9" x 6" (23 x 15cm), five pieces 5" x 6" (13 x 15cm), seven pieces 6¼" x 6" (16 x 15cm).

5 For the tab at the end of the drawstring, cut a piece of fabric, 3½" x 6" (9 x 15cm).

To stitch together

1 Fold the main piece in half, right sides facing, bringing the side edges together. Pin and stitch to make a tube.

2 Machine stitch a line all around the base circle, ½" (1.2cm) in from the edge. Snip up to the stitching line at regular intervals all around the circle.

3 With right sides together, pin and baste the base circle into the bottom end of the tube. Stitch and clip the seams to fit.

4 Make a hem along the top edge of the bag, taking a turning of ⅜" (1cm), followed by a second turning of ⅝" (1.5cm). Baste and stitch close to the edge of the hem.

5 Make the drawstring tabs as follows: with right sides together, fold a fabric piece in half lengthwise. Stitch down the long edge to make a tube, then turn right side out. Turn under the seam allowance to the inside of the tube along both raw ends. Baste and press flat. Machine stitch all around the tab, close to the edge. Make all 14 tabs in the same way.

6 Fold each tab in half and pin it along the top edge of the bag to make fixed loops, each projecting 1½" (3.5cm) above the edge. Space them evenly, with the different lengths randomly placed. On the outside of the bag, attach the tabs with freehand cross-stitches along their edges; on the inside, slipstitch them in place.

7 To make the drawstring, sew the two strips of calico together along one short edge, right sides together. Press the seam

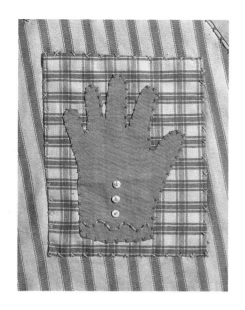

allowance to the wrong side along both long edges of the strip. Fold in half lengthwise, wrong sides facing, so that these turned edges meet. Stitch all along the strip, close to the edge and through all thicknesses.

8 Thread the drawstring through the tabs along the top of the bag. Pin, then stitch the ends together.

9 Make the end tab in the following way. With right sides facing, fold the piece of fabric in half, bringing the short edges together. Stitch along two sides. Turn right side out and press the seam allowance to the inside along the open edge. Push the ends of the drawstring inside the tab and stitch close to the edge to secure.

To work the design

1 Trace the glove shape on paper to make a pattern piece and use this to cut out a glove from a scrap of fabric. Turn under ¼" (5mm) to the wrong side all around the piece, snipping curves where necessary. Baste all around the edge. Work a row of tiny cross-stitches on the glove for cuff detail and decorate with three tiny buttons.

2 Cut a 6" (15cm) square from a contrasting fabric scrap, turn under ⅜" (1cm) all around, baste and press. Place the glove diagonally on the fabric square and baste in place. Work evenly spaced cross-stitches all around the glove shape to join the pieces together, as well as to decorate the patch.

3 Make the other patch motifs in the same way (see page 96). Cut them out of fabric scraps and add buttons and cross-stitches to decorate. Cut rectangles of contrasting fabric to back each shape. Cut enough fabric to leave a border all around the shape, remembering to allow for ⅜"(1cm) hems on each edge.

4 Cut a few smaller patches to arrange among the larger ones and turn under the edges in the same way as before. Arrange the patches at random on the bag as required, pinning, then basting them in position. Stitch the patches in place with evenly spaced cross-stitches worked along the edges.

5 Remove the basting stitches.

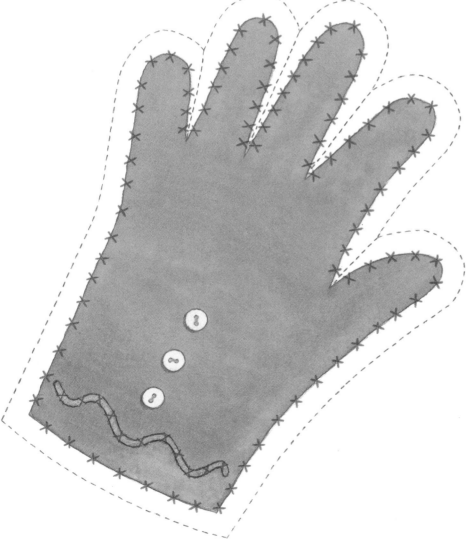

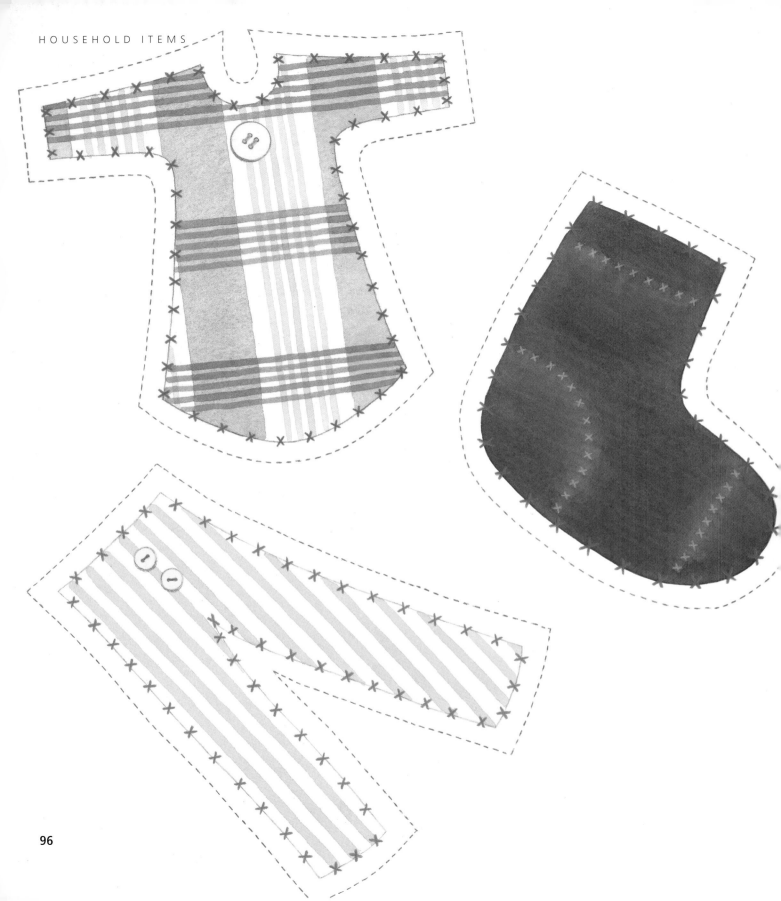

Patterns & motifs

In this chapter you will find a host of extra motifs to use, both as an alternative to some of the designs found in the earlier chapters and also for your own projects. There is a choice of different alphabets that can be used with monograms and samplers; a wealth of delightful miniature motifs from animals and flowers to hearts, keys, and crowns; and finally a selection of borders, medallions, and corner motifs.

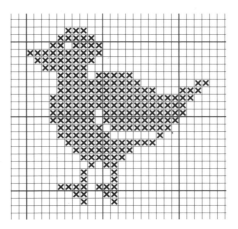

alphabets & numerals

See Samplers on pages 64–79

Here and on the two following pages you will find three alternative alphabets to use when working the samplers and the pillow featured in the chapter: In the living room. The numerals can be worked onto the Napkin Rings (see page 51), and you can use the larger numbers to decorate the Crib Blanket (see page 36). The alphabets and numerals can be transferred onto either a larger, or a smaller grid. This will increase or reduce the size of the finished motifs, enabling you to create an alphabet to the size of your choice, to complement your own design.

98

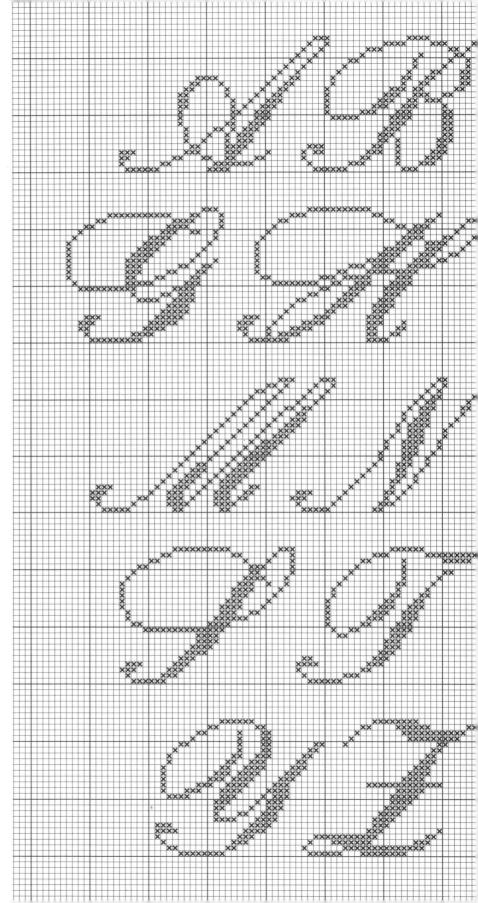

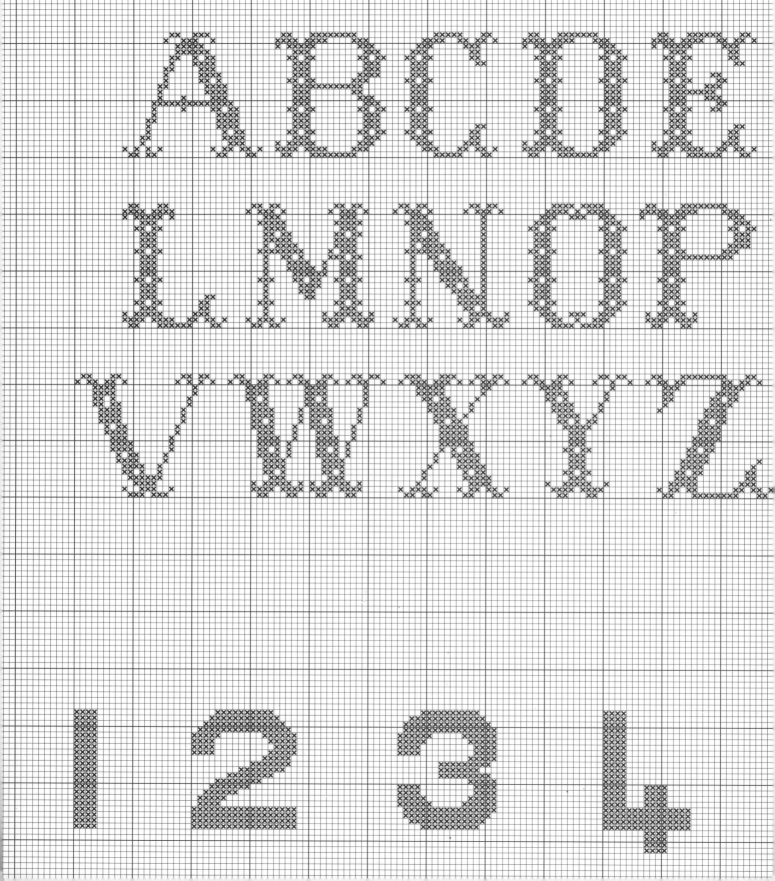

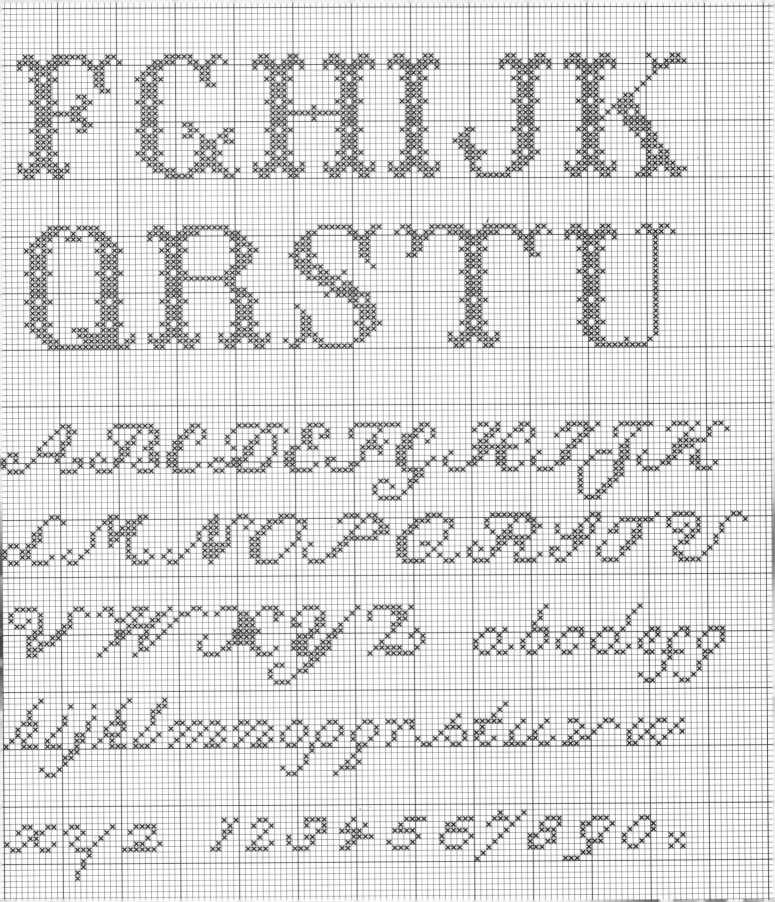

flowers, trees, & mini-motifs

See Samplers on pages 64–79

Choose from this selection of elaborate floral and tree motifs when stitching the samplers and Sampler Pillow, (see pages 64–79). The range of mini-motifs on the two following pages offer a choice of animals, fruit, and flowers, around which you can design a unique sampler of your own. For a regal feel, we have also included some hearts, crowns, and keys, which would be suitable for either the Monogrammed Pillowcase (see page 34), or the Napkin Rings (see page 51).

traditional borders

See Huck Towel on page 86

The borders shown on these two pages will give you a choice of designs for the Blue Panel Curtains (see page 60), the Ribbon Throw (see page 62), or the Huck Towel (see page 86). Be sure to work the borders from the center outward to ensure a complete pattern repeat.

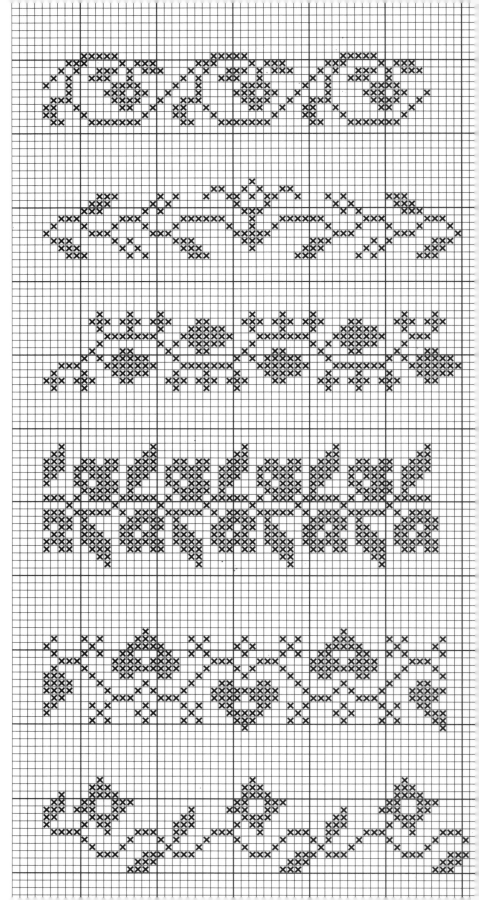

medallions &
corner motifs

See Gingham Table Mats on pages 48–49

These traditional "snowflake" medallion motifs, and decorative corners can be effectively used as an alternative to the one on the Gingham Table Mats (see pages 48–49). You could also use them on a project of your own choice by placing the medallions in straight lines, as borders, or in an allover pattern.

index

acknowledgements

The author would like to thank the following people for their considerable contributions which have made this book possible: Shirley Bradford for using her exceptional technical expertise to interpret some of the antique designs and for charting and originating many of the patterns; Alice Nicol for making many of the projects and samples for photography with great enthusiasm at a moment's notice and with such care and precision and also for her continuing support; Vicky Brooks for designing and making the linen bags; Sarah Clarke for making up projects; Coats Crafts UK, in particular Stephanie Baker in the design department, for technical assistance and contributing the sampler cushion and teacup projects; DMC for supplying fabrics for photography; The Minton Archives for permission to use their designs as inspiration for the shelf edging and teacosy projects; Deborah Schneebeli-Morell for the crown and heart designs for the chair covers; Karen Spurgin for stitching the designs on the chair covers; and The Irish Linen Guild.

For the loan of pieces of cross stitch from their collections: Katrin Cargill, Mary Musto, Deborah Schneebeli-Morrell, Marilyn Garrow, Rebecca Scott Jarrett at Witney Antiques for helping to source the samplers and organising the loan of the church sampler, Kate Shin at Decorative Textiles and Lesley Hackett at Annan & Eskdale District Council for the loan of the school sampler. This sampler is reproduced by permission of Annandale and Eskdale District Council.

For supplying materials for the projects: The Blue Door, Streets, Sanderson, V V Rouleaux, Ian Mankin.